MW00343692

Red Neck,
Blue Collar,
Atheist

Red Neck,
Blue Collar,
Atheist

Simple Thoughts About Reason, Gods & Faith

By Hank Fox

Hank Fox Books
www.hankfoxbooks.com

Copyright © 2010, Hank Fox
All rights reserved.
Published in the United States by Hank Fox Books
ISBN-13: 978-0-615-42990-8
ISBN-10: 0-615-42990-4
For additional copies: www.hankfoxbooks.com
                          www.blue-collar-atheist.com

Table of Contents

Introduction 1

Foreword: Saying Goodbye to Gods 9

Outside the Box ....

1	Sundae Worship	19
2	The Parable of the M&Ms	25
3	Why Beliefs Matter	31
4	The Wellspring of the Gods	47
5	Batman Almighty	67

Morality ....

6	Two People Come Together	77
7	Kind Words	83
8	The Backside of Theft	89
9	Good Without Gods	101

The Price of Faith ....

10	Sucking Up to the Virgin Mary	117
11	Deadline Pressure	123
12	Reading & Reason	131
13	The Mob	137
14	The Downhill Road	143

Freedom, Reason & Science ....

15	In the Nation of Pants	161
16	The Evidence of True Things	175
17	Holes in the Holy	191
18	The Headwaters of Reality	199
19	The Doorway to Freedom	211

Farewell to Unreason ....

20	Uneven Ground	225
21	Hello Mr. Death	235
22	The Black Train	243
23	The Village	255

Into the Future ....

24	Selling Unbelief	275
25	Additional Resources	283

Introduction: Who is this guy?

I grew up in Texas with a bunch of rodeo cowboys.

I wanted to become a veterinarian, a horse doctor, but it didn't pan out. Instead, I ended up working as a carpenter, driving a dump truck and then a soda delivery truck, being foreman of a roofing company, and a lot of other stuff in that same vein.

I moved away to the mountains in the west when I was about 21 and got a job at a pack station (a ranch, sort of) on the edge of the wilderness, where I worked with horses and mules. I was also a teamster for eight years, a real one, driving hitches of huge Belgian and Percheron draft horses on hay rides and sleigh rides in a little resort town.

Somewhere along in there, I thought I might make a good bull rider. I landed in the arena dirt eight times, and got freight-trained by a Brangus bull once, before I changed my mind – but I did ride four of them to the buzzer.

I did a lot of different things in my early years, indoors and out, but I seemed to keep coming back over and over to the outdoor jobs.

Older now, I do a lot of my work indoors – but I can still saddle a horse and find my way in the wilderness. I can hitch up a team and get a wagon safely there and back. I can work cattle in the chute, wrestle a calf, trim a hoof and nail on a shoe, sling bales of hay to a corral full of cows. I can sharpen a knife or hit the bull's-eye with a rifle. I can hook up a horse trailer and pull it safely down the highway. Given time to refresh my memory on the diamond hitch, I could probably still do a fair job of tossing a load onto a pack mule and trekking off into the wilds. I know what it feels like to be bucked off, stepped on, kicked and even bitten by horses.

My neck isn't exactly red these days, but I do carry deep, permanent wrinkles on the back of it from long years spent in the sun – a legacy handed down to me along an ancestral back-trail of farmers and homesteaders, pioneers and pikers, and likely generations of poor white trash scrabbling to survive. One of the stories I got from my granny was that a not-too-distant ancestor was an actual Indian – but since just about every native-born Texan hears that same story, I'm not sure how much credit to give it.

Right this minute, I don't know of a single blood relative who got a college degree. Neither of my parents even finished high school. Daddy drove a dump truck and a city bus, worked as a welder and mechanic, and did a lot of other things to make ends meet. Momma spent most of her time as a housewife and mother, but also held a job in a dress factory for a while and later worked the cash register in a gas station. At the age of 13, I got an Everclear-drinking stepdaddy who was a union painter all his adult life, a man proud of the fact that he dropped out of school after the third grade to go to work.

I have a high school diploma, myself, and even a bit of college, but I too had to drop out and work, and never finished. I am anything but a card-carrying philosopher, a scientist, or an expert in logic. I'm probably not even all that civilized.

But like a lot of cowboys and commoners, I'm also not stupid.

In those years of working hard, I had a lot of time to think. Wrestling a dump truck through traffic, I wrestled with ideas. Sweltering on a roof in the hot Texas sun, I sweated out questions and concepts, jotting things down on torn-off bits of roof-shingle wrapping. Horsing cases of soda pop around on a dolly, I worked things out in my head and marked them in memory to write down later. Over hundreds of tedious days pounding nails as a carpenter, I tried to nail down firm conclusions about the things I'd heard in church and elsewhere. Riding horseback along the dusty trails of California's John Muir Wilderness, looking around me in appreciation at the wildlands and wildlife, I corralled the wild stories running through my head and broke them to saddle.

All on my own, I tried to figure out how things fit together in the real world. In the privacy of my own mind – which is where some things have to stay when you grow up where I did – I started having doubts about religion by the time I was 13.

It took me a good 20 years to carefully consider everything I'd heard – the beliefs of my Southern Baptist mom, my Jehovah's Witness dad, and my born-again fundamentalist Christian stepdad, plus those of all the other people I met or read about who had various religious or mystical beliefs – and compare them with what I knew and all I learned.

Some things began to make solid sense to me. Other things came to sound just plain silly. Considering the state the world is in, some of it even turned out to be a little bit scary.

My goal here is not to lay an exhaustive, reasoned groundwork for why there can't be fragments of Noah's Ark on Mount Ararat, or why Adam and Eve never existed, or why there is no bearded giant sitting on a 50-ton throne of gold up in the sky.

My experience has been that people who are receptive to questioning the family religion have already pretty much figured out that stuff on their own, and are more interested in hearing a friendly voice to help them decide where to go next. The others either can't seem to understand the idea of unbelief or are too busy thinking up triumphant, simplistic arguments for why unbelievers have to be wrong.

Well-accredited authors such as Christopher Hitchens, Sam Harris, Richard Dawkins and others have written more fully and carefully than I could about the WHY of living without gods. This book is more a subjective, one-man's look at the HOW.

Rather than a college course in atheism, this is the equivalent of a grammar school reader, and an incomplete one, and I don't mean it to be anything more. Putting it simply, here are some of the things an atheist might think, and the way he or she might think them, written down from my own experience.

I try to give answers to some of the common questions you might ask yourself – and that others will ask you, such as "If there's no God, what keeps you from killing and raping people when the mood strikes you?" – as you go about riding the trail of a freethinker.

The idea of gods is, at base, a bit of groundless mystical nonsense, but we live in a society so permeated by goddiness that the idea that there might *not* be a God or gods seems perversely even more mystical. Whereas no evidence is needed to claim existence for various magical superbeings, the claim that they might *not* exist is invariably met with fierce demands for proof.

Yet anybody can be a non-believer. You don't have to be a scientist or a highly educated intellectual to understand certain things about the real world. You can be a truck driver, cowboy or carpenter, as I have been, or a cashier, plumber, farmer, auto mechanic, motel maid, laborer, or any of the other countless blue collar professions, and still get there. You can break away from the religious herd and come to your own conclusions about life.

Some of what you figure out will go against the grain of your upbringing. But it seems to me you have to give your deepest allegiance to your own independent mind. Nothing less will allow you to become your own unique self, nothing less will allow you to most completely develop your own unique gifts. And nothing less will honor those who raised you – hopefully to be the best you could be – even if you eventually find yourself disagreeing with some of what they taught you.

The skeptic's journey is a lonely one, and there's no handbook for it. Most atheists I've spoken to are convinced, sometimes fiercely so, that atheism has to be a solitary trip. You have to work things out in your own mind, over a long period of time, to build up to where you start to really understand what religion is, what it does to you, and how little you really need it.

From my own experience, I sort of agree. But darned if there weren't times I wished I could just *talk* to somebody about it. It bugs me that the trip took me 20 years when, looking back on it, with a friend to help, I might have breezed through it in a couple of years and then had the decades since then to enjoy the pleasures and power of a clear mind.

Here, maybe, I can be that friend for others.

Hopefully, I can also share some of what lies beyond atheism. Because I don't think of atheism as a goal in itself – it's more of an escape hatch from the cage of religiosity, out into a larger world that has nothing at all to do with faith.

I will proudly call myself an atheist all my life – but that's partly because it's all some people will understand. Just as my lack of belief in leprechauns or garden fairies would be overwhelmingly important to leprechaun/fairy believers, so my lack of belief in gods is a crucial point to god-believers. They can't help but see this as the only important thing about me.

But "atheism" is really only shorthand for something much bigger. It's a reminder that you can jump the fence of mysticism and go off to find the greener, broader pastures of the real world.

For me, atheism has only a little to do with the negative, the rejection of gods and devils, heavens and hells. Instead, it's more about the positive: freedom. Once you free your own mind from the dead weight of ancient "wise" men, you can finally begin to see the world as it is, and yourself – larger, happier, more compassionate, more centered – as you should be.

There is a saner, more reasonable future awaiting us, a time and place where a majority of people aspire to see things for what they are and then choose to deal with them realistically. It will replace what we have now, where too many of us can't get over believing that some eternity-spanning fantasy makes our own lives cosmically important and everything else – distant stars, a broad universe, and even the civil rights of our neighbors – totally insignificant.

More than anything, I'd like to live in that sane future. Failing that, I'd like to think I can help make it happen.

I'm a guy who once drove a truck, rode a horse, pounded nails for a living. This is how I see the world.

HANK FOX

Foreword

Saying Goodbye to Gods

My dog died.

Don't sweat it – it was more than a decade ago now, and I'm (mostly) over it.

Can't tell you how much I loved the old beast.

His official name was Woodacres Ranger, and he was from a line of champion German shepherd show dogs. But I never even bothered to register him. To me, he was Ranger the Valiant Warrior, my best friend for more than 12 years, and we romped through the heart of the world together.

For most of his life, we lived in California's Eastern Sierra, in a small town at about 8,000 feet above sea level. The trails are rocky, the water is crystal clear and ice cold year-round, and the wildlands thereabouts are filled with black bears, coyotes, uncatchably quick mountain bunnies, and all manner of smells and sights to delight an energetic dog.

We went for hikes along those mountain trails twice a day for just about the whole of his life. I liked to stroll along and savor the sights and sounds, Ranger loved to gallumph the trails and splash in the crystal creeks.

It was during those years that I worked as a draft horse teamster, shepherding tourists on summer hay rides and winter sleigh rides. Ranger came along on most of them, running alongside my big horses, ton-weight Belgians Duke and Dan or Percherons Esther and Jim. He loved to run fore and aft of the wagons or sleighs, exploring, and then climb up onto the driver's seat with me when we stopped to rest. The guests always loved him, my lanky, big-eared, big-nosed, big-footed happy boy, but he had eyes only for me. He was a compass needle and I was his North Pole, and nothing could keep him from me.

Out one night on the streets of my small town, a pack of dogs came charging out of a dark side street and straight for us. I shoved Ranger behind me and crouched down ready to lay into them with fists and feet, but they veered off and vanished into the night. Someone asked me later, "Why would you do that? Isn't he your guard dog?" and I answered, "No, he's my *guarded* dog. Anybody tries to hurt him, they have to answer to *me*."

He sometimes bit me hard enough to draw blood when we were playing, his greetings after the shortest of separations left claw marks on my chest and arms, he took up too much of my bed at night, he filled my couch and easy chair and carpet and truck seat with his ever-shedding dog hair ... and I couldn't possibly have found it any more endearing.

Can't tell you how much it hurt when he died.

I was 45. I was sorta quiet and numb for a couple of days afterward, being all manly and adult about it. But on the third day, home by myself, I suddenly found myself lying on the floor in a half curl, pounding the carpet with my fist and howling like a 5-year-old, "I want my dog back! I want my dog back!"

Whoa.

Like I say, I'm "mostly" over it.

But I learned something in the midst of getting over it, and it's worth relating here in trying to describe what it's like to become an atheist.

In twelve years, Ranger wove himself into my life as closely as anything could be. A lot of who and what I was, was bound up in him. He was with me in the truck in almost every mile I drove, he was with me for those scenic mountain romps, he was with me on trips to the nearby hot springs, he was with me on the wagon rides, he was with me for hikes at *this* place, and *that* place, and all those other places. I spent large amounts of my day, every day, in playing with him, petting him, talking to him, hiking with him, traveling with him, caring for him, thinking about him, even talking about him.

And then one day, he was gone.

After the first intense shock, weeks or months in length, I discovered a series of lesser shocks waiting in ambush over the next several years. Eventually, I understood I was being forced to peel Ranger out of my life one little bit at a time.

I cried about losing him in private at home. But then I had to grieve all over again at each place we frequented, each place that held memories of him.

Went out to where we used to take the hay rides, cried. Strolled out along the nearby creek where we used to hike and climbed up on the log where we crossed, cried. Stopped at a mountain meadow frequented by deer and crossed by a stream, a favorite hiking and picnicking spot for both of us, cried. Passed by a place we used to live, cried. Stopped to look at a flat rock along a mountain stream where he used to hang his toes over the edge and look down into the water, cried. Drove down a highway where he used to aim his nose off the edge of my pickup bed to catch the rapid wind, cried.

In a particularly strong example of what I'm talking about here, it was fully two years later when, for the first time since Ranger died, I came up to one of the places where we had often hiked.

In a town 40 miles south of where we lived, Ranger and I had this one trail along a canal where we loved to spend time. We'd roll up under this big cottonwood tree and eat lunch in the truck, then stroll down the length of the canal for a mile or so, crossing at a bridge and then strolling back. Ranger got to stay wet and cool on the hot summer days, I got to amble along and woolgather, and it was a timelessly perfect moment, every time.

And here I was, two years later, there at the canal, but without my Ranger. Two years later. I pulled up to the base of the spreading shade tree where we always parked, got out of my truck, took a look at the canal stretching off in both directions and the trail alongside it ... and burst into huge painful sobs for the loss of my dog.

Ten years after, just this past summer as I write this, I

stopped on the north shore of Lake Tahoe, where Ranger and I lived for several months, and I stepped out onto a beach where we illegally and delightedly romped every night ... and cried.

What I realized is that when you lose someone you love, you have to say goodbye to them not just at the moment they die but at every crossroads of your life and theirs. They are bound up into a thousand daily moments of your self, and you have to deal with the pain and confusion of losing them at each of those moments. Every act of the day, every near and distant spot on the road of your life that you formerly shared with them, in each of those times and places you have to give them up all over again.

At each crossroads, grieving must take place and be done with.

But this book is not really about death. It's about life.

Pay attention now: In becoming an atheist, I'm not saying you'll feel grief for your missing god – quite the opposite. What I'm talking about is what seems to me to be an unavoidable difficulty of becoming an atheist if you come from a religious background – even a moderate one.

In exchanging the mode of faithistic thought for something more comfortable and rationally satisfying, you might still face a lengthy process before you get the last shreds of goddiness out of your head.

You might recognize fully the emptiness and unacceptability of goddy belief, you might conclude, rationally and intellectually, that your parents' religion (or any religion) can no longer satisfy your reasoning mind ... but it may still take a while to get free of it.

In the same way that Ranger became a part of my thoughts, religion has become a part of yours. In becoming an atheist, every intersection of religion with your life and mind must be examined, thought about, and released.

This can be a time-consuming process.

Lacking any sort of guide, and having to keep the whole chore mostly to myself, it took me a good 20 years to get all the goddiness, all the superstition, all the last suspicions and questions about religion, out of my head. I finally realized – and it was a moment of brilliant light, I can tell you, as positive in its direction as losing Ranger was negative – that I was completely free to be me.

Getting religion out of my head was a beautiful, intense emancipation. The sheer awesome clarity that came to me after that, the peace that descended on me, is not something I could easily describe.

It wasn't the peace of supposedly knowing some holy book was the ultimate answer, if I only gave up enough of my questioning mind to accept every word of it.

It wasn't the elusive peace of believing I'd done every ritual and abasement correctly, that I had scraped and bowed and sacrificed enough that some god would mercifully refrain from killing my loved ones and might even let *me* into eternal paradise.

It was the peace of understanding that, while there might be quite a lot of the world unknown to me, there was nothing purposely concealed. There was nothing "man was not meant to know." The whole of the universe was this honest, trick-free place that I myself could come to understand, with the only limits being *my* limits – of intelligence or energy – and not those imposed by the hallucinatory scribblings of Bronze Age shepherds.

I discovered that there were no all-wise holy men who talked to powerful but secretive gods in ways that were denied to me. There was no magic ritual I needed to perform each day in order to avoid burning in fire.

There was no mystical superbeing looking down in prissy, embarrassed fury every time I got an erection. No mean-spirited creator of the universe taking down my name in purse-lipped concentration each time I wanted to crack open a science book. No small-minded, vengeful holy telepath glaring into my mind and angrily noting my every traitorous, blasphemous, independent thought.

There was no *threat* built into the universe, no lightning-wreathed fist waiting to smash me for making the slightest misstep.

There was absolutely no demand that I give up some or all of my mind to human vultures – priestly con men there to transform natural fears and functions into carrion to feed upon.

Yes, I am still afraid of death, and of loss. But I no longer have to be afraid of life, or of living it.

This is freedom you cannot find in church.

It's only part of what awaits you, as you make this journey.

HANK FOX

Thinking Outside the Box

HANK FOX

1

Sundae Worship

I think all the various religions are like different flavors of ice cream.

Go into your local ice cream shop and you'll see dozens of flavors – enough of them that you can agonize over the choice between one and the others.

But they're all ice cream.

Likewise, religions are different enough that people not only agonize but go to war over which flavor is best.

But if one ice cream has more nuts than another, one has swirls of chocolate while another has swirls of strawberry, one has fudge where another has maple, they're all still just ice cream.

Likewise, if one religion has confession while another

has auditing, one has virgin birth while another has a god who popped out of a crack in the earth, one has a pope while another has elders, they're all still just religion.

Most people are not as adventurous at sampling religions as they are at sampling ice cream – they get the flavor their parents or neighbors have. Probably not because it's what they themselves would like best if they had the choice – it's more because we're all told the other flavors taste bad or are deadly poison.

Maybe it's also because there's no 31 Faithers where you can see all the different flavors displayed together – a place where you can see people talking and laughing and picking the "wrong" flavors and yet surviving afterward to talk and laugh some more.

In the ice cream store, you can choose any flavor at all and most people will respect you for it. They might crow about their own choice, about how much better it is than what you chose, but they won't think less of you for it. If they pick Black Walnut and you pick Maple Nut Crunch, they might poke fun at you, but no more than that.

They won't kill you for it. They won't go to war over it.

If you pick the wrong religion, though, there have been plenty of places and times in the world where you were put to death by the government or murdered by your neighbors. There are places in the world *today* where that happens – places where your own people, your own family, will *kill you* the minute you try to choose some other flavor.

And what happens on the day you decide ice cream is not enough? What happens when you find you want something *more* than that sticky-sweet glop – something more nutritious, more flavorful, more varied, more healthy?

If you go to an ice cream store with friends and you choose no flavor at all, the people around you might crack jokes about it, but they'll still respect you. They might even admire you.

But if you choose no religion at all, there were (are) places and times where you could be (still are) killed for it by religious people.

Even in the sectarian United States, having the wrong religion, or no religion, is enough to get you mistrusted, even hated, by some people.

A study in the U.S. in 2006 found that atheists were disliked and mistrusted – and people wouldn't want their kids marrying one, either – more than immigrants, Muslims, homosexuals, or any other group named.

No less an authority than the 41st president of the United States, George H.W. Bush, denied that unbelievers were even citizens. In Chicago, Ill. on August 27, 1987, Bush Sr. reportedly said "I don't know that atheists should be considered as citizens, nor should they be considered patriots." It was just that kind of ignorance that got people killed in plenty of other places and times.

For these and many other good reasons, having no religion is a *lot* more dangerous than picking the wrong flavor, or no flavor, of ice cream.

People don't lie to make you choose the flavor of ice cream they think you should have. They don't threaten you with death, or eternal torment, if you choose the wrong flavor. They don't tell you you're not a citizen or a patriot, or that you're otherwise unacceptable in society, if you don't choose "right." They don't brainwash and terrify children with the idea that if they choose the wrong flavor, they'll be burned forever in a pit filled with monsters.

But plenty of deeply religious people do all these things and more. And they do them as a matter of course, so that the people doing them think they're not only perfectly natural, but *good*.

So I swore off.

At about the age of 13, I started to notice that ice cream – so to speak – wasn't all that good for you. By the time I was 19, I'd given it up for life. Sometime in my 30s, the last little nagging cravings for it vanished.

At this point in my life, I've been "ice cream"-free for more than 40 years. And it feels really, really good. The confusion and fear brought on by consuming it just melted away.

Now I've graduated to the next level. I'm doing my best to talk other people out of living their lives on all that ice cream.

But of course, we're not talking about ice cream. We're talking about religion.

There are a number of terms attached to those who don't accept religious ideas – agnostic, atheist, secular humanist – and plenty of disagreement both among those who seek to label the unbelievers and those who choose to self-identify under one or another of the terms.

Beyond that collection of confusing labels, though, is a next step, a recognition that, in an era of epidemic-level mental flabbiness and obesity, our society and our world need more than just for you personally, or me personally, to decide not to eat ice cream. This next step is a kind of Surgeon General of the Mind that says "Not only do I not eat ice cream, but you probably shouldn't either."

That's exactly where I am. Not only do I not believe in gods, spirits, demons, heavens, hells, reincarnation, magical fairies, or giant turtles supporting the flat world …

But I don't think you should either.

HANK FOX

2

The Parable of the M&Ms

T here's this thing deeply religious people do that always leaves me at a loss.

Their basic approach to any mystery that confronts them – and "mystery" here can mean anything from well-known facts that they as individuals somehow failed to pick up, to the complex unknowns of the larger universe – is "If I can't explain it, if *you* can't explain it, it must be God."

The thing that bugs me most about these people is that they're so convinced of their one pat answer that they're not interested in listening to any other, or of questioning the matter further to discover still more possible answers.

They're not *curious* about mysteries, they're *satisfied* with them.

So here's how I like to look at all those things I don't understand right now:

Think about all the candy bars you've eaten in your lifetime – Snickers, Milky Way, Almond Joy, Mounds, PayDay, York Peppermint Patty, all the rest.

If you're like me, you've never been to a candy factory, and you really have no solid proof about how these things are put together. But you could probably figure out the basic scheme of each bar with little trouble.

You start with a sweet, thick ooze, mix it with a handful of peanuts, form it into little bars, dip those bars into molten milk chocolate, and then lay them out on a cool surface to harden. Instant Snickers.

Or you start with a bar of chewy-gooey caramel, roll it in lightly salted peanuts so you coat the entire outside, and then lay it out on a smooth countertop to harden. Voila! Payday.

You stamp out discs of peppermint dough, send them for a swim through dark chocolate, then lay them out on a slick, flat surface to harden. Poof! York Peppermint Patty.

You take a short strip of candied coconut, drop a couple of almonds on top of it, dunk it in milk chocolate, and then lay it out on a slick conveyor belt to cool and harden. Bang! Almond Joy.

See? Nothing to it. No magic, no gods, no super-scientific alien civilizations required.

Ah, but think about M&Ms.

There's this little button of chocolate in the middle, coated with a hard candy shell and then painted with candied color. Or there's a peanut covered with chocolate, then the hard candy, then the color.

And it has no flat side.

There is never a time in an M&M's life when it lies on a cool, smooth surface to harden.

How the heck do they *do* that?

If you've been through the M&Ms factory, you probably know the answer. But I don't know the answer, and in a way, I don't want to know it. In this case, I'm happy with the mystery, content to let it serve as a little lesson about people who are convinced that anything you can't explain must be due to the influence of this deity or that.

Because in this case, though I don't know the answer, I'm sure I could find it out in about five minutes. I could find out just exactly how M&Ms are made.

They make them in the space shuttle, I'll bet, and they spray on the candy coating and the color while they're floating in zero gravity. It solidifies in mid-air, and it has no flat spot because it never touches anything until it's hardened.

Or they drop them from a tower a thousand feet high, and they get sprayed with the chocolate and candy and color as they float down. By the time they reach the bottom, they're cool and solid and go right into the bags.

Or they form them like every other type of candy bar, but they then put them in a jeweler's lapidary tumbler with a fine grit that, over a period of weeks, polishes off the flat side to a perfect roundness.

They grow them in the Andes Mountains on genetically-engineered mutant chocolate plants, where they're picked by child labor. Hundreds of old guys who look exactly like Juan

Valdez carry them down the mountain with long strings of pack donkeys, and they take them to a factory where thousands of tiny Filipino women making 11 cents a day snip off the stems and paint over the scar with matching colored paint.

Well, it's none of those things. You and I both know it. And those are all fairly mundane answers, with no magic or god-power required.

I don't know how the cheap earphones on my CD player were made, but I know it wasn't magic. They were put together by low-paid robots in a big industrial facility somewhere, and they work by simple principles of physics.

I don't know how my computer was put together, but I know there's no magical elf in the box, no telepathic alien. It's basically a light switch on steroids, programmed by nerdy youngsters hopped up on Jolt Cola and strawberry Pop Tarts until they're so hyper they start to think in computer code.

I don't know exactly how the supermarket door knows to open when I walk up to it, but I'm absolutely certain that it isn't an invisible genie enslaved by sorcery. It's hidden switches and motors and this infrared electric eye thingie that – because I'm on the short side – misses seeing me about half the time.

Physics. Electricity. Ordinary everyday stuff, with a lot of technical skill thrown in to make it jump through complex and useful hoops.

Just because I don't know how these things work is not reason enough to leap at the Almighty Master of the Universe as the answer.

In this case, the answers to these mysteries, though they're not known to me, are known to *somebody*. I just haven't gotten around to looking into them myself.

As to other mysteries, it's just darned amazing to me that a wound on your arm can heal back to be level with the rest of your skin, instead of healing into a ragged little canyon, or bubbling up with new flesh until it forms a large irregular lump. It's wild that there's a totally invisible ray that can shine right through your flesh and bones, and show doctors what you look like inside.

But it's even more amazing, even more wonderful, that there are people – biologists, physicists, other scientists – who know a very great deal about the why and the how of it.

I think it's cool as hell that the puzzle-piece way that Africa and South America seem to fit together is because they *did* once fit together, and even cooler that there are knowledgeable people – geologists – who can tell us how and when it happened.

But even if the experts don't know every little thing, is there reason to believe such things are magic? Reason to call on Holy God Jehovah as the One True Answer? Reason to stop looking for the *real* explanations because the fluffy mystical one seems good enough?

Nope. Just because you don't know the answer does *not* mean that it's evidence of God, or gods – or witches or demons or mind-reading aliens from Planet Z.

Out here in the real world, things just don't work like that.

M&Ms are not made by God.

They only taste that way.

HANK FOX

3

Why Beliefs Matter

Why do beliefs matter?

"I didn't think the gun was loaded."

Need I say more?

But of course I will. Because this is important.

Beliefs matter because they have real consequences. The stuff in your head has an effect, through your actions and reactions, on the way you live your life in the real world. However slight, it *always* has an effect.

And the stuff in the other guy's head matters because it has an effect, through *his* actions, on the way *he* lives in the real world.

And that affects you, too.

Let me back up a bit to do some stage setting:

Every bright young person sooner or later wonders "What if this is all happening completely in my head?"

Once you realize that whatever's out there isn't exactly what you're seeing – that the image in your mind of the speeding truck approaching you is really just photons bouncing off that might-be truck and then traveling across fairly empty space to strike your eye, getting translated there into chemical and electrical signals that travel up sloppy neural wires to enter the perfectly dark bony box in which your distant, lonely brain resides, incomprehensible signals that then get translated by your soggy gray matter into some sort of mental interpretation of that original speeding truck – well, you have to entertain a doubt or two that your experience of the world is completely real.

What if the truck is really a duck? What if the worst you'll experience is a surprised "Quack!" when the two of you collide?

What if the truck is not really there at all?

And yet few of us are willing to just step out in front of it.

The idea that the whole world might be happening exclusively in our heads has some obvious dangers. If the truck is real, suddenly you might not be.

Given a choice of "It's all happening in my head" and "There's a real reality and I and everyone else live inside it," most of us choose some version of the second option. Not always because we're totally convinced but because ... well, life goes on, and if you can't figure out the *real* answer, you go with the half-assed answer, the best one you can come up with, until something better comes along. You realize in the end that there's some process by which photons, sloppy nerve signals and the workings of our largely unknown brain conspire together to produce something that seems to us to be real.

Yet we always wonder ...

The truth is, given the choice of "all happening in my head" and "real reality," we don't have to choose one or the other. Because both are right.

The things of the world are completely real. And it's all happening in your head.

The fence

Imagine a long fence.

On the far side of the fence is the real world itself. The entire outside universe, doing all the things it does: the dog that barks in the night, the tree that falls in the forest, the whole universe of Other that exists independent of you, uncaring of you, largely even unaware of you.

On the near side is the place you live, the place where resides the totally subjective experience of You. This is the private viewing room in which an audience of one – you – watches the outside world roll past.

Pressed up against that fence are your sense organs:

Your skin – to feel the breeze, to detect movement and vibration, to explore texture, to sense pain, to experience caresses, to note sharp and dull, rough and hot, cold and pinch and whack and sting.

Your ears – to hear loud and silent, shout and sing, buzz and hoot, doppler up and doppler down, symphony and cacophony, sweet vocal tone and nerve-jangling ringing phone.

Your tongue – exploring wetly to find hints of salty and sweet, peppery and sour (and dark chocolate!).

Your nose – snuffling eagerly at the fence, picking up from the other side hints of rose and cinnamon, baked chicken and Old Spice, horse and hound and soap and skunk.

And above them all, your hungry eyes – gathering huge amounts of data by digging into the visual feast of the other side: the million colors, the dark and light and grainy and smooth, the this way and that, the fast and the slow and the come and the go.

Behind those sense organs, well away from the fence, in perfect darkness, near-total silence, immense isolation, your sneaky brain sits and builds models.

Your brain builds models of the real world, models that are *not* the real world itself. Yes, there is a real world out there for it to build models of, but the models are not the real things. That does seem to leave plenty of room for uncertainty about the whole mess.

So here comes this truck. A White Freightliner hauling a 53-foot refrigerated trailer filled with frozen fish. Total weight, 30 tons. Glossy deep blue cab with "Haxton Trucking, Kirby, Indiana" on the doors and metal-flake gold script lettering on the rear panels saying "Hoosier Daddy." Twin stacks belching diesel smoke in a black swirl, it's headed your way at 60 miles per hour.

And here you are just stepping off the curb, building models in your head.

This particular model can be a fairly faithful one which includes the true details of the truck, speed and estimated weight and so forth, plus a cautionary dollop of memory based on all the thrown baseballs, swinging fists and skateboard-riding friends which have in the past impacted on various parts of your body.

Or ... it can be a bad model that imagines the truck as a vision of perfection with which you seek to merge, a psychedelically beautiful bloom of colors and sounds that strike you as totally groovy, baby.

Which model will allow you to continue to live your life (and go on to leave offspring with some of your same traits)? And which is likely to result in a loud, nasty splat?

Further:

You have a bump on the side of your face. It's come up in the past 6 months or so, and where first there was a tiny mole, it is now a quarter-inch across, mottled purple and brown, and irregular in shape.

Your husband is staying late at work night after night. There's also a beautiful new secretary in the office.

Your 10-year-old son has cerebral palsy. A man on TV tells you Jimmy can be healed if you only pray hard enough ... and send in money.

You read the numbers on your lottery ticket and discover you've won $8 million.

The woman you want to spend your life with says yes.

The things you believe, the models you have in your head, have complete power to affect the ways in which you approach these situations. They also have great bearing on what happens afterward.

You go to a dermatologist immediately, or you ignore it. You set a trap for your husband, or you give him the benefit of the doubt. You flip the bird at the televangelist and change channels, or you send him money. You cheerfully call all your friends, or you fearfully hide your lottery fortune from everybody. You grab your girl in your arms and dance around the room, or you coolly say "Well. Good."

Your reactions depend on the models in your head for dealing with those situations. Reactions depend on what you believe.

The real world may give you lemons or lemonade, and a great deal of that you have no power over, but – given what life hands you – the models you hold in your head are hugely important to how well or badly you're able to deal with each new situation.

Here's the thing, though: A bad mental model almost always gives you wrong answers. You get useful answers, right answers – if at all – only by accident.

Given any type of real-world problem, threat or opportunity, if your model is 10 percent off, or 50 percent off, or 100 percent off, you'll fail to come up with a useful reaction in some similar degree.

If the model in your head says the gun isn't loaded, but it is, somebody could die. If the model says the truck is no threat, perhaps because no driver would dare hit a pedestrian, and you step off the curb, you might find yourself waking up in the hospital ... if you wake up at all.

If the model says a big purple bump on the side of your face is nothing to be alarmed about, you might end up like my too-tough cowboy friend Tom, who died less than 6 months after he finally *did* go to the doctor.

On the other hand, if the model says you should act coolly

toward your fiancé and wife, you might miss out on huge amounts of silly, laughing joy, or even find yourself in divorce court in a year or two.

Get it? There's a real reality out there. And then there's this model-building mechanism in your subjective little head that tries to understand and react to it. The two have to work in tandem for you to operate in the real world as effectively and safely and happily as possible.

Out in the real world, a speeding 18-wheeler is a deadly juggernaut that can wipe out you-the-pedestrian and come away with nary a dent. If the model in your head recognizes that, you're less apt to get hit and killed.

Out in the real world, a fast-growing purple bump on the side of your face is nothing to ignore. If the model in your head takes that into account and sends you to the doctor as soon as you notice it, you're more likely to survive, less likely to force funeral and medical bills onto your wife and kids.

A real-world-based mental model gives you better answers. Cheaper answers. More efficient and effective answers. Bad mental models kill you, hurt you, cheat you, fool you.

The good thing, if you have a bad model in your head, is that you can learn better. The real world almost-but-not-quite forces you to. If all your answers are wrong answers, you wise up, based on real-world (sometimes painful) feedback, and think up better ones. Or you lapse into sullen withdrawal, refuse to change, and accept the consequences that are forced on you.

Again: You don't have a lot of say-so about what happens out in the real world, but you do have some choice about how you see it, how you react to it, what overall effect it has on you. You can't change the fact that huge ocean waves are powerful and dangerous, no matter how much you might wish or pray or fantasize them to be different, but you can, with the right mental model – and a surfboard – choose to ride them.

Selling to others

In the everyday details of our lives, how do these things work out?

Given the fact of real reality, and the fact that we're all sitting up in our heads cranking out these mental models, and then the fact that we're able to communicate with each other, it was inevitable that at some point we'd begin to share with each other our private mental models. In fact, a considerable amount of what a lot of us do is an effort to enforce or coerce our own mental models onto others.

Businesses do it: Budweiser is the king; it's second to none. With the patented Ab-O-Sizer, those pounds and inches will just melt away, with absolutely no effort on your part. The New York State Lottery – Your Chance to Win. You've come a long way, baby (and by the way, there is no evidence that smoking causes cancer)!

Politicians do it: For a brighter future, vote for Tommy Ray Taylor. We're winning the War on Terror. This bill will end the practice of elected officials taking money from lobbyists. I did not have sex with that woman for six consecutive hours in a beach-front cabana in Belize.

Individuals do it: The check is in the mail. If you really love me, you'll say yes. Of course I'll respect you in the morning. No, seriously, you look great.

Preachers do it: You can't get into Heaven unless you give up your doubts and devote your life wholly to Jesus. God has lifted the veil of protection from America because of our tolerance for homosexuality and abortion. The Church is deeply saddened by these assaults on innocent children, and will do everything in its power to see that incidents like these never come to light again.

If Madison Avenue – or the White House, or your new boyfriend – can get you to fully adopt the mental models they supply you, they can get you to agree to anything, and you'll pay any price to do it. Urged on by mind-pictures of immense wealth, gullible buyers spend billions of dollars on lottery tickets; only a handful win the big money. Millions upon millions of people take up smoking, because of how cool and adult it is, and find later they can't quit. People buy $80,000 cars that are very little different from the $20,000 ones, and they're *happy* about it.

Seeing the future

There's more. Model making comes into play in the deepest areas of our own personal lives. For instance, one of our great powers as humans is predictive foresight that allows us to foresee upcoming conditions, so we can take advantage of all the good things to come and avoid all the possible bad ones.

But to be able to use foresight, you have to have models in your head that are close to what's really out there in the real world. If the models in your head don't line up with real world conditions, foresight doesn't work. Good things happen to you only by accident, because you're not able to make workable plans to cause good things to happen. Bad things spring themselves on you without you being able to do anything to head them off.

It's easy in such a situation to become convinced that all of life is about luck, or fate. The daily surprises of life constantly convince us that we're powerless and weak and forever in need of help from the mystical forces of Lady Luck, or God.

This is precisely why less-educated people are more prone to believe in things like luck and fate, predestination and gods. Lacking the knowledge that would help them understand more about the real world, their superstitions are all they've got to hold onto in the uncontrollable storm of their lives.

The fatal flaw of mystical belief is that it actually reinforces itself: If you believe in the mystical, you suffer the negative side effects of having a bad mental model ... but suffering from those negative impacts causes you all the more desperately to *need* to believe in the saving power of the mystical, because you know that you yourself are powerless. You keep hoping and praying your "luck" will change soon and things will get better, but meanwhile you go on doing everything just as you've always done it – you keep gambling for money instead of working hard and saving, you keep marrying the same type of abusive guy rather than taking a long, hard look at yourself, you keep praying for a sudden miracle to make your life better rather than figuring out a workable long-term plan to see that it does.

Peasants and potentates

Model-making extends to the systems of government we choose, and that we then come to be affected by.

In open societies, for instance, the individual gets to make his own evaluations, decisions and mistakes but also gets to profit from his successes. He gets quick feedback – personal success or personal failure – on his mental models: If he prospers, he keeps the models; if he fails, he adjusts them and tries again.

But in autocratic societies, evaluations and decisions are made by a dictator, king or priestly class. Social or business or religious models are enforced-by-force on the average guy by a leader who wins both when he's right *and* when he's wrong. Whatever happens, the king makes out okay. The little guy, on the other hand, pays the bills, picks up the pieces, or serves as cannon fodder in the king's war.

If the man on the street can't make his own decisions, much less profit from them, he stops trying to understand things, stops trying to figure out better ways to do things. The model in his head defaults to something like "I can't understand any of this crap. I ain't even gonna worry about it anymore; let those smart bastards figure it out if they can." He ends up living in a state of permanent sullen discontent.

It's easy to understand why open, democratic societies, which allow individuals the freedom to succeed on their own efforts, make huge leaps in economic and scientific progress, while autocratic societies – where success for the common man is totally disconnected from how hard he works, or how well he comes to understand a particular problem, or how creatively he invents a solution to it – stagnate and fall behind. A slave society simply can't compete with the drive, imagination and creativity of free people.

The success of each culture, and every individual, depends less on unquestionable myths and hidebound cultural practices and more on what's really true. Accurate mental models – real-world-true beliefs – matter. They matter to the individual, and they matter to the entire society. Always.

Yet anytime people talk about competing religions, you inevitably hear this: "We should respect each other's beliefs."

But people vote their beliefs. They raise their kids by those beliefs. They run for school boards based on those beliefs. They buy things based on those beliefs. They try to impose those beliefs – regarding contraceptives, scientific and medical research, the necessity of wars, the use of public funds for religious charities, who each person is allowed to have sex with, sometimes even how you're allowed to die – on the other people around them.

The question is: Do you and I have to allow the "beliefs" of others to override our own values and practices? When those beliefs move out of *their* heads and into *our* lives, do we have to give way?

It seems to me the very foundation of personal freedom is that we *don't* automatically have to respect others' beliefs. Especially when they're not respecting ours – such as all those times when their beliefs include the belief that the rest of us should be less free to think our own thoughts and live our own lives.

Science and sacraments

Finally, model-making affects even our largest social choices – whether we as an entire people will cleave to reality-based philosophies or wishful ones, and how those choices will be carried out among and upon us.

Most religion is about protecting and spreading the

authority of particular mental models. Go into any church you ever saw, and ask "Does it really matter what I believe?" The answer will be some form of "Yes! It matters that you believe *this*, the stuff *we* believe."

Religious modeling is closed-source. You're not able to make changes; you accept it as it is, or they throw you out. Nobody you know was ever allowed to write an extra chapter to the Bible or Koran. There's room for interpretation, but there is almost no place for input to the basic models.

Science, on the other hand, is about extending our mental models to evolve progressively greater effectiveness in the real world. Science takes a *lot* of independent data from a *lot* of different sources to form its models, and those models remain forever open to improvement.

"Open to improvement" doesn't mean scientific models and conclusions are blithely doubtable. The changes, when they do come, are additions and refinements to already-useful ideas. The process is akin to that of healthy young people who decide to take up weight training or running – starting from a physical foundation that's already strong and healthy, they aim for better and stronger.

And become stronger they do. Just as, daily, science does.

Because the mental models of science are open-source. Anyone can add to scientific models. There are hundreds, maybe thousands, of people alive right now who helped write extra chapters to the "book" of science, and textbooks are updated often with new facts and discoveries. In science, there are even awards – the Nobel Prize, for instance – for the people who write these new chapters.

In religion, the prize for people with radical new ideas is to be cast out. Shunned. Disfellowshipped. (Except in those times and places where their neighbors delighted in torturing and killing them.)

Scientific models remain fluid, forever subject to improvements, because scientists want the *models* to be right more than they want the *person* – any particular scientific authority – to be right.

The authority for the Catholic Church, the infallible Pope, is considered by devout Catholics to be literally incapable of being wrong. By contrast, not even the most famous scientist can escape the disagreement, even the gleeful ridicule, of his fellow scientists the very day he makes a pompous, unsupported statement.

The personal price

In the end, it's better to believe true things.

It's better to examine and update your beliefs and knowledge whenever possible, rather than clinging to outdated, defensively rigid mental models.

It's good for *you* to evaluate and learn about the real world, and build your own mental models for what's true and what's not.

It's always a mistake to simply accept the beliefs of some authority, whether holy book, holy man, car salesman, corporate pitchman, radio personality, or even elected public official, without examining and evaluating them in your own mind.

The reason is simple: The very fact that we live in the real world means that bad mental models always have negative side effects – side effects that may only subtract some of the joy and ease from your life, but that *can* injure or kill you (while your anointed leader, if that's who you're trusting to provide the mental models you use, sits up on the hill in a big house, safe and rich and insulated – by you – from all his mistakes).

You only get these two choices: You're an adult – someone who controls his/her own life – or you're a child, a ripe victim for the next parasite that comes along looking for a meal.

In any case, whether it's something you figured out on your own, or a false belief foisted on you by someone else, it is *you* who will suffer, in your own life and in the lives of your loved ones, the consequences of mistaken beliefs.

Better if those consequences result from your own free choices and beliefs, so you can learn better – so you can change your behavior and get better results next time – rather than from the rigid commands or commandments of some supposed authority.

HANK FOX

4

The Wellspring of the Gods

S
ome years back, I came across a magazine in a bookstore with the cover teaser, "Why Religion?" I practically snatched it off the shelf, excited that I was about to learn what makes us religious.

I was disappointed. The writer took the easy way out by focusing only on the history of religion – where it might have started, how it continued, where it spread. In the end, he didn't answer the question at all. He wrote at length about the "where from?" of religion but never touched on this other thing I think is more important, the "how come?" – the "why" of religion.

The history of religion doesn't tell you anything except that a sequence of events happened. It doesn't tell you why people allowed it.

Religion didn't just spring up as some sort of independent living thing at its distant point in history and then magically continue forward into the present on its own. No, it had to travel through those several thousand years in some kind of vehicle, and that vehicle was the human brain.

Religion happens in the individual mind, and nowhere else. The "why" of it can only be found there. Billions of times, one person at a time, generation to generation, religion found root *for some reason* in the mind of a living human being, and was carried forward through history in each new generation.

Recent writers have talked about a "god impulse" – of our brains being "wired for god." They come right out and say that goddiness is built into us like hunger, or laughter, or knees. They hint that we should probably just give ourselves over to it and be glad about it. "If our brains are wired for god," they pretty much say, "then there must be a god who wired us that way. Anybody who doubts it should just give up and let the natural faithiness come through that silly agnostic shell they've built up."

Argh.

Simultaneously righter and wronger than that religious history author, they get the active site of religion correct – the human mind – but they get the mechanism for it (deliberately, of course, because they have a vested interest in their own little sectarian pitch) all wrong.

Yes, it seems to me, religion is a result of natural functions of the human mind. But it ain't inevitable – the existence of any number of decent, well-adjusted atheists, agnostics and humanists proves it. Besides which, "natural," like the salespitchy term "organic," doesn't always mean good. Black widow spider venom is as "natural" as fresh-squeezed orange juice, but you won't find me pouring myself a cold glass of it every morning.

Yet these people will reel off arguments like: a majority of humans throughout history have believed in gods, billions of people alive today are devout, humans have an inborn sense of awe and mystery, on and on. Therefore, religion is "natural."

But such an argument for religion as "natural" is pretty much the same thing as saying that rape is "natural." After all, human males are aggressively sexy beasts and throughout our existence as a species have practiced rape. Rape is part of history, folklore and even religion, and it features in all sorts of popular entertainments and private fantasies even today.

But does rape meet our approval as "natural?" Maybe during the Mongol invasion it did, but it doesn't at *this* moment in civilized history. Today we think of sexual assault as a flawed side effect, a perversion – a wrong, even harmful use – of natural attributes. What we consider normal loving relationships become more difficult both for the victims – the women (and men, and children) who suffer from it – and the victimizers.

Religious mysticism isn't exactly rape, but you see my point: "Natural" attributes can be tweaked off in unhealthy directions.

Though it arises from natural attributes, religion can still have negative effects on the normal rational thought of both the people who spread it and the people affected by it. In the religious mind, objective rational thought and the ability to distinguish between fact and fantasy – in the vein of religion, at least, and probably in many others – become more difficult.

This is why you'll hear countless times during your lifetime of religious con-men – whether evangelists, investment schemers or political manipulators – pulling the wool over the eyes of believers, despite being painfully obvious phonies.[1]

But back to "why." I think there are some fairly simple answers.

Why Gods?

Anthropologists and psychologists might have the best chance of figuring out the answer to this, but as they have never, as a body, put forth any such explanation, it leaves it to us to figure it out on our own.

I think I can make some pretty good guesses.

Putting it in simplest form: We have gods because we have parents.

You grew up with at least one very powerful being in your life – a source of punishment and sustenance, of pleasure and pain, of fearful angers and gentle affections, someone who could solve your every problem, someone who gave you love and tenderness but who was also incomprehensible and frequently capricious, someone of vast power who nevertheless often chose to withhold your moment-to-moment fulfillment unless you were "good."

From the instant of your birth, the impression that was burned into your unformed mind by that powerful being,

---

1 *In my time, Jim and Tammy Faye Bakker were the prime Christian manipulators, and a more blatant, shameless pair of sticky-sweet fakes you'd have been hard pressed to find in public life. After being dethroned from their position of influence and Jim sent to prison, the wonder was that they'd ever been able to gull anyone with their on-cue tears and transparently phony pleas for donations. Yet the two had an audience of millions. When they vanished, the manipulations were picked up seamlessly by many others.*

your mother (or father, or both), is as permanent as your belly button. Later, in adulthood, the place in your head formerly filled with the constant, powerful presence of Mommy or Daddy comes to be occupied by god-belief.

I'd bet most people are even grateful to have that emptiness filled. Rather than growing into the next phase of adulthood, the demanding state of independence and responsibility, they can continue to enjoy some of the comforts of staying a child. Who, in this scary world, wouldn't like to believe that somebody bigger and smarter is handling all the really tough problems?

More, here's something that probably *is* wired into our brains: For a period of time when we're still kids, we automatically accept the things trusted people tell us.

When I was about 8, one of my brothers warned me about the dreaded lettuce bug, a pale green insect that would, if you swallowed it, burrow up through you and *eat your brain*. I asked him about it years later, and he didn't even remember telling me. He'd made the story up on the spot just to tease his gullible little brother. But meanwhile, before finally figuring out the story was complete BS, I'd spent years carefully and fearfully washing every leaf of lettuce I ever put on a sandwich.

For a significant portion of our young lives, most of us are literally unable to doubt what mom and dad – and sometimes older brothers – say. Some large part of our young brains are keyed to automatically believe supermom and uberdad.

A survival trait proved out over our species' history in a hostile world, it's something easily perverted into religious channels by our culture. Tap into that uncritical open circuit at any point in history and you have a continuous reinfection of every new generation: If your mother tells you God watches and judges your every act, and if her mother told her, and so on back into prehistory, the family religion starts to seem like a natural attribute of the entire species.

Except it really isn't.

Why an afterlife?

Allegedly a latecomer addition to early mathematics, the zero took a while coming probably because it was hard to imagine it being useful. Pre-zero accountants, calculating the number of sheep coming to market or jugs of wine to be loaded onto a ship, must have had a tough time with the idea that "nothing" might be worth thinking about.

Zero sheep, zero jugs of wine ... hard to picture.

Even harder to picture zero Self. Every facet of our awareness and thought has to do with the concrete fact that we're here and alive. We humans simply have a hard time thinking about not existing.

We have almost as hard a time imagining the non-existence of our loved ones. Our memories are so good they stay real in our heads practically forever. More than 20 years after my cowboy friend Tom died, I can still "hear" the pitch and intonation of his voice repeating some of the characteristic things he'd say. More than 35 years after my daddy passed away, I can clearly picture his thin, craggy face.

When we burn firewood, we know that chunks of wood go in one side of the process and something totally different – cold ashes – come out the other. Firewood doesn't have an "after-wood" where it's still somehow wood. Burning *destroys* wood, ends it, turns it into this totally other thing, which is not-wood, nothing-like-wood. Most of us feel the same way about animals, and experience no emotional connection between the meat on our plate and the real critter it once was. Death *ends* plants and animals both. They don't have an unseen essence that hangs around somehow.

But our human selves are a lot more personal. There must be more than the simple end that everything else comes to.

The very words we use to talk about the subject have traps built into them.

First, the fact that you can talk about a thing at all short-circuits disbelief. If you can talk about unicorns or flying saucers, werewolves or chillywhoopers (whatever those might be – I just now made them up), the very fact that we have nouns to attach to these non-things makes them more familiar, more believable. Their existence is at least arguable, in the sense that immediately, in the moment of naming such a thing, a pro and con becomes imaginable. Even a person who had never heard the word "chillywhooper" might be instantly willing to argue that such a thing could exist – some part of us insists that there wouldn't even be a word for it if it wasn't somehow possible.

The fact that we can talk about a thing sways us to believe in it, but I suspect the *way* we talk about it affects us even more.

If you say "Bob is tall" or "Bob is out jogging," you clearly picture Bob being or doing. After years of this, even if the thing you eventually say is "Bob is dead," you're still saying "Bob *is*," and it sneaks into your head the idea that Bob is still somehow doing or being.

Maybe "dead" is just another state of existence, like "asleep" or "away." Bob exists in the somehow-or-other state of deadness. Instead of going from Bob to no-Bob, we go from Bob to Dead Bob. Bob's a little different, but still there, still with us. We're a little foggy on the details, but hey.

If Bob still exists, it's only a short step to imagining places for Bob to be. The no-longer-here-but-still-somewhere Bob leads us to postulate – and populate – heavens and hells, souls and afterlives, as places for Dead Bob to inhabit.

There's another important point here: If you believe in an afterlife, your personal relationship with Bob continues. But if you don't buy into this afterlife stuff, the love that you have for the recently deceased Bob has nowhere to go, no way to be expressed. All the things you didn't tell him and do for him when he was alive, all the things you would be telling him and doing for him if he was still alive, they sit hopelessly at the roadblock of his death.

This is powerful motivation for belief. Living day to day, how many of us truly express the depth of affection and respect we feel for each other? How many of us ever get around to apologizing, or thanking, or paying back all our personal debts? With the parting caused by a loved one's death, some measure of guilt falls on us right along with the grief.

But what if fatherly old Pastor Rick tells you that all the stuff you didn't get said, all the things you didn't do, all the debt-paying and favor-returning and last-wording, could still be done ... through him?

Wouldn't you know it? Churches and shamans of all sorts (including 'psychic' con men) are right there to bleed off that load of guilt and grief. They provide a connecting link to the no-longer-here Bob by assuring you that your beloved friend or relative is still alive, somewhere, somehow. Bob hears you, Bob knows you care, and you'll even see him again ... but only through *them*.

The fantasy of an afterlife, with a church as the go-between, provides a tidy mechanism for siphoning off the love we feel for each other, and feeding on it.

If you believe what they say, live as they tell you to live, keep on giving them your time and money and allegiance,[2] you get to keep active the connecting link between you and your departed love, thereby avoiding the sorrow, the guilt, the pain, the loss.

It's a con job for which many of us can't help but feel grateful.

Why mystical beliefs at all?

Religion is recreated in each believer. All of us possess the complex of mental habits that can feed the mystical impulse. When that impulse is encouraged by religious pitchmen, reason, which takes independent effort, comes a distant second.

But even without religion, we're susceptible to the lure of the woo-woo.

As we build our mental models of the real world, we guess at the parts we don't understand, trying to fit new things into a framework of stuff we already know. If the new stuff seems to fit, even if we have to invent still more new stuff to make it fit, we're comfortable with it for the moment.

But the less knowledge you have, the more guessing and tweaking you have to do. Eventually, it becomes impossible to separate the guesses and tweaks from the real knowledge.

---

2   *Compared to these guys, an honest buzzard is practically the Tooth Fairy.*

It's even worse if you're forced to start with the flawed guesses and misbegotten tweaks of the previous generation. If you grow up in an already-goddy society where a lot of the important questions already have wrong answers, you don't have much chance of going back to zero and figuring things out on your own.

If a lot of what you already "know" is mystical models forced on you by your own people's history and culture, and if nothing else in your pre-literate, pre-scientific, pre-reason era matches it even slightly, you're pretty much forced to accept that it's magic, evil spirits, witches, the Little People, or the will of the gods.

Fundamentalists the world over instinctively know this, and discourage education and curiosity almost by reflex. If you can keep knowledge away from your victims, they have no choice but to swallow what you tell them.

Besides all that, complexity itself is mysterious. Anything complicated fits all too easily into this "it doesn't match anything I know, so it must be magic" category. So much so that nature itself – the realest stuff there is, but also damned complex – can seem to prove the existence of the supernatural.

Really, though, is that anything more than a lack of imagination? This fault in reasoning is so common there's even a fancy name for it – the Argument from Ignorance or the Argument from Incredulity:[3] If I can't imagine any other answer, it must be God.

What *is* "natural" is this: It's natural for us to discover, as we become adults, the confidence that learning brings. The

---

3 *Or my own Argument from M&Ms.*

more we learn and know, the less we feel powerless and lost. We can come to understand that more and more of our questions will eventually have answers, and we can develop the ability to continue on even in the face of uncertainty, secure that the answers will come in time.

Religion, by contrast, insists that some things remain unknowable forever, and that many questions should not even be asked. I'd be surprised if this wasn't something that showed up in human history, as a way to control others, almost as soon as we could talk to each other.

From the victims' side, maybe most of us just fall into a kind of confused silence as we discover we'll never be allowed to ask questions. But giving in to the mystical impulse is just that: giving in. Call it personal laziness, call it necessary submission to overwhelming social pressure, it's the willingness to sink back into childhood's safe helplessness, to give up the adult-like belief in our own power to get answers.

Besides, there's this mystical expert on your team, right? You might never understand a thing he says, but if he's on your side, all the spooky mystical questions are covered and you have nothing to worry about. You hope.

And meanwhile, he's got you by the short hairs. Speaking of which ...

Why priests?

Picture an early tribe with a single great hunter getting the best food, hottest women and driest part of the cave to sleep in. Fellow tribesmen left out in the cold, horny and hungry, would naturally be jealous of all that. But only those lucky enough to grow up to be big and strong and dangerous would have any chance of overturning him and taking his place. The wimpy, weak ones would stay cold, hungry and horny.

But if a certain tribesman was wimpy, weak, cold, hungry, horny and *clever*, he might figure out a way to use the fear his fellows displayed in the face of natural forces to give himself a lift up into greater influence.

Say he finds a way to get himself associated in tribal minds with the awesome powers of nature: Lightning strikes and kills three of the tribe, and this fellow tells everyone that the lightning did it on purpose because they weren't paying enough attention to the wishes of Wonga, the spirit of the lightning. Which he knows because he got it from Wonga Himself.

Facing an overriding fear and lacking the ability to argue with the guy – we're not talking critical thinkers here, after all – they could only accept it. Voila, instant shaman.

Wotz of the Ten Wives might have the biggest spear and the strongest club arm, but if little Gurg *commands the lightning*, there will be times when Wotz himself bows to the will of Gurg.

Shifting from respect for muscle power to fear of this other kind of power might take only a few sessions of mystic mumbling during rainstorms and constant dire warnings of bad things to happen. Because bad things always happen. The guy who placed himself protectively between those possible bad things and the nervous potential victims might easily get their attention and allegiance.

And anytime he failed: "What the hell, it's not *my* fault the tribe's best hunter got killed by lightning. I *tried* to intercede, but Wonga told me Wotz was bad for hoarding all the hot chicks, and decided to zap the selfish bastard anyway. It was all

I could do to keep Wonga from killing the lot of us. The rest of you might do well to listen and obey next time I tell you what Wonga says. And hey, how about all these suddenly-available babes Wonga has provided us? Woo-hoo!"

Having stumbled on a way to use people's fears, to control the source of those fears, a shaman-wimp would gain non-physical power, power over their minds – spiritual power.

Fairly obviously, there would be no shortage of powerless, sneaky, slightly mad little tribesmen. Aging or handicapped tribal members might gravitate naturally to the position just out of a desire for continued existence.

European history shows the technique works: Even physically powerful warrior-kings had to worry about being toppled from power if they ignored the demands of the shaman-wimps of the church.

It goes on even today – fear continues to be the primary motivational tool of priestly powers. No U.S. president in recent memory has failed to court the favor of our own culture's shaman-wimps ... because it would cost him dearly if he appeared to ignore them. Evangelist Billy Graham – a guy who knew little or nothing about foreign policy, economic matters, education or any of the thousand other things a president must be required to know – stepped into the Oval Office in 1950 to meet with Harry Truman, and for the rest of his life enjoyed an open door with every U.S. president.

Why churches?

For we humans, power and money are like birdseed to birds – toss it out in the open and something always shows up to feed.

Like birds, we humans show up to eat on the first day the

seed appears, but unlike birds, on the *second* day we start trying to figure out how to get more seed. We organize to make it all happen automatically.

Churches are one result of that trend to organization, a streamlined businesslike form that gives as little as possible in order to gain as much as possible.

In one sense, a church is like a chicken farm. It probably looks to the chickens like the farmer is their friend and servant. He feeds, he protects, he gives direction and order.

But he also harvests, just as churches harvest. Oh, boy, do they harvest. They give out chickenfeed and get back fortunes.

Yes of course priests have to eat. But do they have to live in castles? Palaces? Their own private country? I know of at least one person who'd say No.

Church money goes waaaay beyond simple grits and biscuits for a kindly pastor, or even the necessities of charity. Anyone who's ever seen a picture of the Vatican (a separate little country owned by a church), or driven past one of the soaring castle-like cathedrals that seem to exist in every big city in the world, has to figure out that literal truckloads of money – tax-free money, at that – are involved. And not one dime of it permanently bound up into those showy palaces will ever get within ten miles of the poor, the sick, or the hungry.

Birdseed to birds. The money is there, the priestly class notices it, end of story.

Driving around the neighborhood where I lived in a northeastern city a few years back, I started to notice that the area was well-supplied with churches. In fact, once I started looking, it began to seem there were more churches than any other single enterprise. Just out of curiosity, I went down to the county offices to check the tax rolls and discovered there were, within a mere 2-mile radius of my house, close to 80 properties that were either churches or church-owned.

Churches! More than schools, more than government offices, more than dry cleaners and hardware stores, more than convenience stores. More than gas stations, or pizza parlors. More than *Starbucks*.

Yes, they were many different denominations, but they were also all churches. You wouldn't think "spiritual guidance" would be a greater need than coffee and donuts, or education, but apparently it is.

Worse, estimating the value of these properties based on their locations, and also knowing that they're owned by churchly organizations and forever tax-free, it's clear the dent they make in the local economy is staggering.

Churches get more than money, though. They get entire human lives. They get power.

Power: Priests and churches get to insert a commercial on the day of your birth and the day of your death, and on just about every day in between they get to tell you how to live, how to act, how to marry, what to eat, what to wear. And most of all, they get to tell you *not to leave*. Not to let others leave.

Birdseed to birds. Even assuming there was some pure moment at the founding of every religion (which I *don't* assume), there came another moment when one or more of the bright boys on the inside said "Hey, we could really get people to *do* stuff!" Forever after, "God's will" perfectly coincided with their own needs and appetites.

Everything from admonitions to be good – and penances when you're not – to urging you to give some of your income to the church, to demanding you wear a certain type of clothing, hat, hairdo or even underwear,[4] to expecting you to show up on a certain day and time, to creating specific god-approved rules by which you're expected to live and die, those are all deliberate applications of churchly influence.

For all of the history during which we've had churches and priests, they really have existed to run people's lives. It's all for the peoples' own good, of course. (Well, usually. Some of the time. Isn't it?)

Speaking of just one narrow issue, I think of the hundreds or thousands of years during which many Catholic families believed it was their duty to turn over one of their sons to the church. I toss that into the mix with all the recent stories about priests molesting altar boys, and I shudder to think what sort of private appetites the church came to cater to, and how long it went on.

Considering the Catholic Church in the past few years has done everything it possibly could to keep the story from coming out, or admitting anything when it did come out, there is little doubt it continued for a long, long time. And it wasn't just that nobody inside the church thought to stop it, or to warn parents that it might happen – on some level this stuff took place, century after century, with full conscious support of powerful insiders.[5]

---

4   *Yep. Believe it or not, the Mormon Church recommends "temple garments" – the so-called "magic underwear" – for the faithful to wear.*
5   *Including, as we now know, the current Pope.*

The price of "believing"

Some people are not just religious but hyper-religious. You must have seen them out there on the street, screaming about Jesus and waving pictures of aborted fetuses as you drove past. Or walking around with sandwich signs that said "Repent!" Or driving cars literally covered in hand-written Bible verses and bumper stickers.

There's something painfully, obviously broken in such people. It's not hard to see that extreme forms of religiosity are a kind of mental illness.

Even as I write this, the news carries the story of a Jehovah's Witness woman who gave birth to twins and then bled to death from hemorrhaging[6] while her family stood by, refusing to the very end to give doctors – who were begging them – permission to give her a blood transfusion.

Her family will mourn her loss for decades to come, and two beautiful babies will grow up never knowing their mother. The children might even suffer intense feelings of guilt later, believing themselves to be the cause of her death – especially if some stupid relative tells them "Your mother gave up her life for you!" All for an obscure silly belief, based on one or two isolated Bible verses, that she must refuse a simple medical treatment that saves millions of lives every year, and would have saved hers.

Think of the people you know who have religion, and think about the varying degrees of it among them. Comparing those who are mildly religious with those who are extremely religious

---

6   *Emma Gough, 22, died October 25, 2007 at the Royal Shrewsbury Hospital in Shrewsbury, Shropshire, England, after suffering a hemorrhage following delivery and refusing supplemental blood to save her life.*

and looking at how it affects both types of lives, it's not hard to see a clear correlation between extreme faith and nuttiness.

The Jim Jones[7] cult in Guyana didn't gather together and drink poisoned juice because they wanted to bring about an end to war.

The Heaven's Gate[8] cult didn't commit mass suicide as a reminder to everyone to vote, or buy American.

Those Christian-sect parents you read about a couple of times a year who kill their critically ill children by withholding medical care from them don't do it because they're worried about the shortage of doctors and medicine for poor people.

They do such things because they're wacky as hell.

And in my mind, at least, there isn't any clear dividing line between the extreme, nutty forms of religion and some sort of healthy, "safe" kind. One cigarette (or even fifty or a thousand) probably isn't going to kill you, but that doesn't mean it's *good* for you. Even a beginning smoker finds himself less fit – you don't find cigarettes in the lockers of champion athletes. In the same way, even the milder forms of religiosity skew your sense of the real and make you less able to deal with the questions of everyday life.

Beyond the case of any individual person, the sad fact is that out in our larger society, over the entire world, there is an active army of religious promoters, recruiters and apologists who constantly hector us, via every form of mass communication, to become ever more religious. Just as cigarette manufacturers

7   Jim Jones was the Christian creep who duped more than 900 of his followers into a mass suicide in Guyana in 1978.
8   A bunch of young victims who fell for a line by a crazy old fart who told them they were going off to live on a comet. On March 26, 1997, 39 of them were discovered dead.

were able to do (something we eventually passed laws against), they work to sway us into more and more religiosity. Unlike cigarettes, though, religion comes with no warning label.

There's also a strong and pervasive social context that supports and defends the right to the daily public practice of these types of irrationality. Even though it was trophy-level dumb-assery,[9] the story of the mother who died refusing a blood transfusion after giving birth to twins was reported as straight news, with no hint of criticism, censure or even question.

Even the most extreme of religious believers are seldom criticized by other members of their faith. Perhaps fearing the critical public eye will fall not just on the nut-cases but on their everyday ordinary selves, the non-extremists seem always willing to provide safe cover for the extremists. The best they can manage, when push comes to shove, is that the freaky ones are not "real" Christians, or not "real" Muslims.

All of this has a price. Growing up as we do in a religious society, that price is hard to see clearly, but I think it's higher than any of us can easily imagine. It warps every aspect[10] of our lives and society.

The poison taint of Jim Jones-type craziness is on all of us, to the exact degree that we allow this stuff into our thoughts and into our lives. We like to think that Jim Jones, like Hitler, was a pure-evil one-of-a-kind, but lots of people have a 5 or 10

---

9   *C'mon, you know it is. If you're on the cusp of cheating two little babies out of ever knowing their mother because you have some nebulous objection to a simple, proven medical procedure already accepted by experts the world over, BEND THE FRICKIN' RULES.*

10   *Speaking of monetary matters alone, try to imagine the dollar value of 80 church properties in a mere 2-mile radius in the heart of just one small-to-average city – $35 million? 50? 100? – and then extend the view nationwide or worldwide and think about how far that amount of money would go in providing playgrounds and schools, or hospitals, or permanent college funds for the local kids.*

percent share of his same disease. Some have more than that –
I'd bet money there are more than a few who, walking around
looking normal, voting and raising children, driving on the
same roads as everybody else, even serving on school boards
and operating children's day care centers, get the full dose.

Maybe the taint of religion on individuals is not that big a
deal, but when it blankets entire cultures, nations, the whole
world ...

It starts to get more than a little spooky.

5

Batman Almighty

I realized something recently. An important metaphysical fact.

There is no Batman. None. Batman does not exist.

There will surely be those who argue that I can't say this with authority. That I can't make such a claim unless I search the entire universe to make sure that the real Batman isn't hiding somewhere.

And there's probably no formal logical proof that anyone prone to argue such matters would accept. I could also never convince a single devout Batman-ite. (Except there probably aren't any.)

But I can prove it to myself, and to other reasonable people. There is no Batman. And I know it by a process I call the Ten

Thousand Clues.

As a matter of record, a guy named Bob Kane took credit for creating Batman in 1939. He made Batman up, right in his own head. And all those actors who portrayed Batman on TV and in the movies casually spoke of Batman as if he was nothing but a comic-book character.

Let's get real for a second: In this world of guns where even small-town cops wear body armor, do you think a caped crusader could survive? Considering that there are plenty of people who can hit a rocketing clay disk in the sport of skeet shooting, would a cable-swinging "superhero" last more than a few weeks of attempting to swoop down on heavily-armed drug dealers? As a secretive character who prowls around crime scenes at night, he might just as likely be shot by police officers themselves.

Besides which, if there was really a Batman, the tabloids would have him and Robin on the front cover in the first month, speculating in lurid and suggestive terms on the private lives of the tights-wearing Caped Crusader and the (snicker) Boy Wonder.

Considering how much media attention the "subway vigilante" got some years back, a secretive private crime-fighter wearing a costume would be on the front page of every newspaper and TV station in the country, for as long as he tried to do the thing, and the paparazzi would outnumber the criminals. Batman would outsell the latest blonde pop music sensation.[11]

Groupies and reporters would stake out the roads, alleys

---

11   Hell, there would be entire photo-essays based solely on close-ups of his "package."

and woods around Gotham City (if there was a Gotham City, which there is not), and would, in about a week, find the secret tunnel where the Batmobile comes out of the Batcave.

And you can just bet your patootie that any real Batman would be in court demanding some of the money made off all the comics, movies and action figures that have depicted him.

He'd need that money. Because the minute everyone found out who he was, all those bad guys, some of whom would be sure to have friends in Congress or the White House, would sue the cape off him for assault, stalking, great bodily harm, and anything else they could come up with. Even deep-pockets Bruce Wayne would be scrambling for cash.

Not to mention the case that the underaged Robin would make in later years after all those repressed memories of violence and night escapades started to resurface.

But Batman – not just any "bat man" you might make up in your head, but that specific trademarked character who has a Batcave, drives around in a Batmobile, fights crime in Gotham City, has a butler named Alfred – isn't real. Batman doesn't exist, and never did. Lots of other stuff gives away the fact of his non-existence. So much so that nobody rational would really argue. These are some of the Ten Thousand Clues.

It's the same for Santa. Even though you were probably a devout "Clausite" when you were a kid, it didn't take a lot of deep research for you to discover that there is no Santa Claus.

All of us figured it out about Santa. We peeked in and saw mom and dad wrapping presents and tagging them "From Santa." We saw all those "Santas" at the malls and knew they weren't the same guy. Our classmates told us they'd found out the truth about Santa. We grew up, probably before the age of ten, and learned that there was no Santa at all, anywhere, ever. None. Even though we hated the end result ("No Santa? Awww."), we saw the Ten Thousand Clues, and we came to the only conclusion possible.

Every halfway bright child comes to *know* there is no Santa. Every child comes to *know* that there is no Batman.

The same procedure works for disproving the existence of other fictional, supernatural or mythical creatures. Because most every adult eventually comes to *know* that there are no werewolves, no vampires, no fairies, no magic beans.

They don't just theorize about these things in some vague way. They don't withhold judgment on the existence of magic beans while they patiently wait for more evidence.

They *know*.

And the exact same procedure works for disproving the existence of gods. Even the one you believe in. Yeah, even the capital-G God of the Christians.

If, that is, you can get someone to actually voice one or more concrete, indisputable facts about him. If he exists, if any believer can confidently say he exists, there has to be *something* knowable – and known – about him.

Speaking of which, there's probably no better "proof" there are no gods than the nature of the claims made about them.

Over and over in every religious debate, people trot out their tribe's particular holy book, clutching it to their breasts as if it was some kind of perfect, infallible guide to all of reality and a gushing fountain of unquestionable, exact Truth. Yet even the most glancing inspection of any of them finds unbelievable, overblown fairy tales starting on page one. Talking snakes? Virgin births? Flaming chariots flying across the sky? A guy with the head of a crocodile? Magic spectacles? The entire universe popped into existence in less than a week? Come *on*.

Preachers defend this silliness through strained arguments that sound less like somebody after true facts and more like a high-priced lawyer grasping at every least scrap of doubt in order to defend a celebrity client against a murder rap.

The problem for priests is that real things are connected. Real things prove themselves by slapping you in the face with their realness. You don't have to invent or imagine things to support that realness. You don't have to concoct elaborate just-so stories ("Noah took only young animals, which were smaller and easier to fit onto one boat.") to try to explain how they somehow exist despite not having tangible evidence. Ten Thousand Clues and all, real things just *are*.

When you walk into a church, what do you see? Elaborate decorations, fancy hats and clothes, and one or more people willing to talk – shout, weep, rage, gesticulate, speechify, exhort, chant, sing, argue, sermonize, reenact and illustrate – endlessly about their version of what's real and true.

But no solid clues. Seriously, where are the *facts*?

On the other hand, if you walk into a museum ...

More than 65 million years after the last big dinosaur died, in addition to myriad bits of esoteric evidence linked through a dozen different major fields of science, we have fossilized dinosaur bones. Sixty-five million years beyond the day the last one walked on Earth, we know the shape of their actual skulls. We know what they looked like. We know how they moved. We know what they ate. We have their teeth, their horns, their eggs, their poop. We've seen their *footprints*.

This is evidence as plain as a tractor idling in a field is evidence of a nearby farmer. It's evidence a child can see and understand. Though they lived *more than 33,000 times farther into the past* than the pivotal story of the Bible, we have the kind of proof of dinosaurs – Ten Thousand Clues and more – that anybody can walk into a nearby museum and see.

You don't have to take anybody's word for it, even that of the people who run the museum. You just walk in and it's all there, no shouting or weeping necessary. Nobody demands you "have faith" in it, or throws you out if you don't.

If a car salesman told you a Humvee got 75 miles per gallon, you'd automatically disbelieve him ... *until* he proved it to you by driving 75 miles on a gallon of gas. Even then you'd suspect some slick scam – you'd call several friends to come in and witness it too.

Because most of us have to have more than just a slick pitch – more than just talk, talk, talk, however loud or intense it might be. In fact, the faster and more flowery the sales pitch, the less apt you are to believe it, right? Because if you're more than 10 years old, you already know that the weakest arguments are the ones delivered at top speed and loudest volume. The salesman tries to distract you with bright lights, flashy colors and emotional intensity in order to keep you from noticing the lack of real substance to his claims.

But you want something more than what a salesman says. You want evidence. Proof. Some kind of independent corroboration of concrete facts.

That's not even being skeptical, it's being *normal*.

That same type of *normal* demand for evidence and proof, the type of proof that slaps you in the face and doesn't have to be explained and defended by juvenile-sounding fantasy stories or legalistic bombast, we should expect that of everybody. Including priests, holy books and the claims of true believers.

Of course, there's nothing anyone can say that would convince the truly devout. But they'd never listen to *any* argument, much less hang around to hear about – or objectively think about – the Ten Thousand Clues.

Just because they refuse to think about it, though, or just because there are millions of them, or even because they enjoy a temporary historical majority, that doesn't mean they're right.

They're wrong.

Just as we know there is no real Batman, we know there are no real magic wands, fairies, faith healers, mind readers or magical Ruby Slippers.

And as near as I can tell from the Ten Thousand Clues, there are no real gods.

But that's a *good* thing.

HANK FOX

Morality

HANK FOX

6

Two People Come Together

I meet you on the street. Something happens.

It's the most basic of human interactions.

Anything could happen in that meeting. Both caught up in our own thoughts, we could simply fail to notice each other. We could see each other, nod absently, and walk on. We could see each other and scowl and walk on. We could stop and have an extended conversation about any of a million little things – you could tell me what a nice day it is, and I could give you a tip about how to make your lawn greener.

Darker things could happen. I could insult your girlfriend, and you could take offense enough for us to end up in a knife fight. Swaggering out of Dodge City saloons on opposite sides of the street, we could recognize each other as rivals, open our coats to reveal matching Colt .45s and have a Wild West shoot-out right there and then, and both end up plugged and bleeding on the street.

This "coming together on the street" could happen literally on the street, but it could also happen in the boardroom of a multinational corporation in Greece. It could happen in a kitchen in Cut and Shoot, Texas, as a man and his wife yawn and scratch and wait for the coffee maker to finish. It could happen in an airport in London as two jet-lagged travelers pass in a corridor. It could happen anywhere.

But it's not where the meeting happens that I'm interested in, or even the happenings at the meeting, it's the after-the-happenings.

Because every time two people come together, something lasting has a chance of occuring – and in my view, in the long run that's a lot more important.

Working together

Say there are only two people in the world. And there's work to be done, a lot of it, in order for the world to be a better place to live in. Say we've gotta get a whole winter's worth of firewood in.

Under what conditions is all that work likely to get done? If both are working to their fullest? Or if the two are working to less than their full ability?

If you wake up this morning ready to help, but I get up irritated and tell you what a worthless slug you are and how you never do your share, that probably will have a negative effect on your willingness to participate. If I tell you instead that you're the best partner a man could ever hope to have in this important work and I'm constantly amazed at how much I get done when working beside you, that will probably have a positive, energizing effect.

Scale it up. Imagine there are three people. Four. A dozen. A thousand. Six million. Six billion. Scale up the vital work to be done – not just the firewood, but all the other stuff required to keep 6 billion people alive … and carefully not destroy the planet at the same time.

Again, under what conditions is all the vital work likely to get done? The same answer: It's most likely to get done if everybody, or most everybody, is cheerfully willing to dedicate their full capacity and range of talents to it. It's *most* likely to get done if we help each other be as good and productive as we can be.

In the end, it doesn't really matter how many people there are. Every interaction between people can be boiled down to a simple picture:

Two people come together …

… and something happens.

We part unchanged

At the end of our meeting, you're neither diminished nor enlarged. Ditto for me. I'm okay, you're okay, nothing's different. This is not a bad result. We feel every bit as confident and complete as we did when we started, and we can both of us still do our part of the work.

If neither of us places very much importance on our interaction, it may have little or no effect on us. Going into this meeting, I might have a grandiose conviction of how wonderful

I am, and you might have your lifelong sense of inferiority, but neither of those would be due to the fact of our meeting. Coming out of this face-to-face, I might still have my smug and lofty view of myself, and you might still have your grinding sense of smallness.

On the other hand, maybe we place great importance on the meeting, but we both simply depart from it unchanged from what we were.

Either way, the meeting makes little or no difference in us. We come out of it just as we were when we went in.

This is the least interesting of the results. Where it gets interesting is in all the other outcomes.

We part with one diminished

How about if I unintentionally take something from you? What if my chain saw kicks back and slices your leg? Or I drop a rounder of pine on your foot. I cough and infect you with a fast-moving virus. You hate my Patsy Cline CDs so much it gives you a pounding headache.

We certainly won't get the work done very fast *now*.

I might be able to do my part, but you won't be able to do yours to anywhere near your previous capacity.

We part with one diminished, one enlarged

I take something from you, but I gain something from it. I become larger, better able to do my part of the work. But you shrink somewhat, become less able to do your part.

I take your lunch money. Now I have more money, but you don't get to eat lunch. Happy at my good fortune of now possessing your money, I might very well work better, cut more wood, than before. But hungry and distracted, your performance will suffer.

Or I sneer at you and tell you what a loser you are for wearing the wrong boots. "Everybody knows the truly studly firewood gatherers wear Tasmanian Devil boots, the choice of Canadian lumberjacks! Haha! Notice my own manly boots, with the Tasmanian Devil logo branded right into the genuine steer hide leather!"

I work with confidence and pride after one-upping you, while you stew in anger because nobody ever told you that you had to have the right boots. Maybe my confident performance will exactly counteract your lessened performance, so there's no net loss or gain.

On the other hand, it's possible it won't. It may be that your performance will suffer *more* than my performance will improve, and we'll have a net loss in work accomplished.

We part with both diminished

After stewing for a while over that crack about your unmanly boots, you pop me in the eye, temporarily blinding me, and I respond by kicking you in the knee, temporarily laming you. What sort of performance are we likely to turn in now?

A pathetic one. I can't see the wood as well, you can't walk as well to stack it, and we're both distracted by pain. We might even quit for the day, or forever, getting in no firewood at all.

But in the best of all possible worlds, something really good happens:

We part with both enlarged

I slap you on the back and tell you what a great friend you are to help me with this firewood; you tell me you consider it a privilege just to be spending time with me. The hard work goes lightly, the time passes quickly, and the day ends with so much good work done it surprises us both.

More practically, I sharpen your chain saw, you give me your extra gas for mine, and we both become better able to cut firewood. You bring over your wood splitter, I pitch in my extra gloves, and we get many times as much firewood cut and split and stacked as either one of us working alone, or even both of us working together but not contributing the gear.

Alrighty, given the obvious effects of the possible outcomes, and given that there *is* a lot of vital work to be done, the question is: Why would you tear down other people at all? Why should we not work to get everybody as productive and effective as possible?

Why not give the people around you respect, assistance, positive reinforcement ... even love?

Duh.

And the next question is: Do you have to belong to a church or religion to know this, or to put it into effect?

Nope. Not at all, not in the least, not a scrap. You only have to know it, and to want things to be better.

Double duh.

7

Kind Words

So here's me, wicked atheist with an evil reputation to uphold, and I have this dirty little secret: I like to give people compliments.

Sincere ones, I mean. Not anything phony, to curry favor, but stuff that I notice that's true, and just as a sort of gift.

Early on, I had to make a deliberate effort to do it – not so much to notice good things about people, but to overcome my natural shyness about speaking up – but now it comes easily.

Nice shirt. You have beautiful skin. Your garden looks really great. I like your hair. That was a good piece of work. Wow, that's one hot-looking Harley! You look nice today. When I grow up, I want to be skinny like you. I read what you wrote and I thought it was terrific. You have an amazing smile. I heard you on the radio and you sounded like an absolute pro. I know you must hear this a lot, but I think you're beautiful. Your little girl is really smart. I can tell you've put a lot of work into your lawn. Whoa, wicked truck – you've got some nice toys, dude. That was a brilliant observation! Your kids are beautiful. You two look really great together. Damn, I can really tell you spend time in the gym. That's the coolest darned painting I think I've ever seen. That was awfully gutsy of you. Your music really moved me. You have the most striking eyes. Thank you very much for your help; it made a big difference.

Part of the reason I do it is that I realized a while back how long compliments stick with you. More than 50 years after, I can still vividly remember a compliment I got from a stranger when I was only about 5 years old (and no, I'm not telling). Even today, I'll feel good about a compliment, sometimes for days.

The really weird thing about compliments is that they cost the giver not one red cent, but they can be gold to the person getting them. You'd think more people would make the very slight effort it takes to do it. And yet it seems most of us don't.

Here's something I believe:

There's a rough sum that can be made of your life at any one moment, a measure of how much good you've done compared to how much bad. I imagine the good and the bad placed on a balance scale from day to day ...

You know the kind of scale I'm talking about? One of those seesaw "scales of justice" that has the two hanging pans you can put weights on so that one side dips, the other rises?

For the thing to stay balanced, for your *life* to stay balanced, if you put a "bad" weight on one pan, you have to put an equal "good" weight on the other. If you weigh down your scale with bads, it will tip down really low on the bad side. If you stack a series of goods on it, it will weigh more heavily on the good side.

This good and bad balance in your life doesn't happen in isolation, of course. The people who know us have their own estimate about where our – and their own – running balance stands, and they react to us based on that estimation.

My own view is that where our own individual scales stand *matters* to our larger society.

To change metaphors for a moment, imagine that there's a bittersweet "flavor" to human society, a blended whole of all our efforts. Every one of us would have *some* effect on that flavor. The ones who do more good things than bad make it a little bit sweeter. The ones who do more bad things than good make it a little more bitter. And the ones who perfectly balance, or those who do nothing much, one way or the other, they help society be more bitter, too – because bitter happens all by itself, whereas sweet is something you have to work at.

There's an echo effect back from our larger society into our private lives. If a majority of us inject bitterness or fail to add sufficient sweetness, we're all forced to live in a progressively more bitter society. Which worsens things even more by making us all a teeny bit less able to feel like adding sweetness.

The bitterness, in case this isn't clear to you, plays out as things like fear, pain, loneliness, tension, anger, greed, stridency, suspicion, and hate.

The fruits of sweetness are things like trust, camaraderie, fun, fellowship, neighborliness, generosity, safety, relaxation, forgiveness and caring.

Just like everything good, the sweetness is uphill and always takes work. Just like everything bad, the bitterness is downhill and is so easy it happens almost by itself.

The great thing about compliments is that they're the exception to the "hard work" theory of sweetness. They're easy. They don't cost anything. But they can add a lot to the sweetness.

You do have to practice a bit to develop the habit of giving compliments, but it gets to be second nature in only a little while and takes no effort at all afterward. A happy side effect, after you learn to do it, is that you're always looking for good things to notice about people.

Try it! The next time you notice the beautiful creamy complexion of the young cashier in the supermarket, tell her about it. The next time a convertible pulls up next to you at a stoplight – assuming you like convertibles – roll down your window and call out "Hey! Cool car!" The next time you see a well-dressed older woman on the street, smile as you pass by and say "You look really nice today."

The only trick to it is that you have to get it into your mind that the compliment has to be, first of all, sincere, and second, a *gift* and not a bargaining chip. The type of compliment I'm talking about is not wheedling, not a currying-of-favor, not the first move in a seduction. The goal of a compliment is to walk away leaving the other person feeling good about himself or herself, instead of feeling they've just heard the first half of a sales pitch.

Guys, this might take a little work on your part to separate the essence of complimenting a woman from that of flirting. The trick is, if it's a beautiful woman you're talking to, you have to give the compliment and then walk away. Women will have the parallel problem that some men will hear any compliment as a proposition. But there are plenty of others out there – parents, children, seniors, friends, coworkers – who are just as hungry for compliments and with whom you won't have the problem.

Developing the habit is tough at first. It takes a while to learn that you're not losing anything by giving. It takes a bit to get comfortable with the idea that it's *okay* to do it. But it becomes a comfortable habit in a surprisingly short time.

And it helps keep the balance on the positive side.

The rule in my own head is: "Anytime you find yourself thinking something good about somebody, tell them instantly. It's a mistake to hold it back."

It doesn't cost you anything. It brightens the day of someone else. It sweetens the society you live in. And it gets you looking for positive aspects of the people around you.

Might be worth a try, huh?

And, once again, you don't have to read the Bible, or belong to a church, to do it.

HANK FOX

8

The Backside of Theft

T wo blocks away from my house, the little store was called Andy's Handy Superette, and it was run by a guy we called Handy Andy. He was a jovial middle-aged man and I liked him.

But I was 5 years old and not yet versed in all the nuances of responsible behavior. So I stole candy from him.

They were called "Smarties" – flat little pastel tablets with concave ends, a dozen or so of them done up in a roll – this was about 1957, so they might have been a penny each, might have been two for a penny. Did the different pastel colors have different flavors? I never could tell. All I cared about was that they were intensely sweet.

I came in with my brothers, who were buying bread or some

such for our mom, and I slipped a roll into my pocket on the sly and ate it later in private. I did it two or three times, the same candy each time, and I never got caught.

Fifty years later, there's no way to fix it, and I'm sorry about that. I feel a sort of second-person fondness for the little rascal I'm talking about, and I don't want to think of what he did as a crime worthy of any great punishment. But the memory of it from my youngest years, viewed now through the filter of my adult morality, aches a bit when I call it to mind.

Not only do I now know what I did was wrong, I know a number of reasons *why* it was wrong. And it has less than zero to do with "Thou shalt not steal," or God, or gods, or anything of the sort.

Among all the other good reasons for not stealing – mainly that it hurts other people – there's one that I think every young person should know but that nobody ever mentions:

Stealing makes you weak.

Seriously.

We have plenty of images of thieves in modern TV and movie culture. At one end of the spectrum, we have the lovable rogues who live by theft but who are really decent people inside – Robin Hoods who are only stealing to help the poor. At the other, there are the cold, calculating geniuses who gather teams of skilled experts together to rob banks of millions and retire rich on distant islands.

And in none of those stories does anybody ever say that stealing makes you weak.

We usually think of thieves as strong. Bad people, maybe, but powerful ones, compared to us. Personal experience with a few thieves leads me to believe that plenty of them probably see themselves as powerful. They're the strong predators, and their victims, the suckers who work at jobs to make money, are the weak prey.

And yet it's nothing like that. In human society, it's mostly the complete opposite. Being peaceable and hardworking is worlds apart from being weak.

I know for a fact that going through school is a lot of damned hard work. I know for a fact that holding down a job for years is a monument to persistence and determination.

People who go to school and have productive, money-earning careers are strong, capable people. They are people who can make plans, work for years to carry them out, and then triumph in the end by completing them. They end up with larger incomes, greater freedom of choice, greater personal independence, greater respect from those around them, stronger families, and even more cool toys than the people who don't.

People who steal from them, on the other hand, even though they may appear the stronger of the two in the moment of theft, are weak. They can't do much at all on their own. They have to have big strong people to feed on in order to survive.

It's like comparing the Budweiser Clydesdales and horseflies. One of them works hard and is universally loved. The other feeds off them but gets – and deserves – no respect.

Just as exercising a muscle causes it to grow stronger, performing useful work throughout your life causes *you* to grow stronger. If you learn how to program computers, for instance, you've increased your store of knowledge, your flexibility, your ability, in one more way, to make a living. You have an extra tool in your mental toolbox. Plus, knowing that you're able to learn useful new things is the fertilizer for ever-growing self-confidence.

If all you do is learn how to steal computers, on the other hand, you've got the one skill, and it leads to ... nothing much. It's as if you decide you want to put on some muscle, but you coerce somebody else to come over and lift the weights. *You* get no stronger, and the next time you need a weight lifted, you have to coerce somebody again, and the next time, and the next, and the next.

By becoming a thief, you become *more* dependent on others, rather than less.

There's a social side-effect, too: If you come to believe that other people can be forced or tricked into supplying your needs, it cripples your ability to relate to people on any other basis.

Stealing makes you weak. And the longer you steal, the weaker you become.

Show me the money

Stealing makes you poor, too.

With the tiniest bit of research, I could probably come up with 50 computer industry people who have become millionaires or billionaires. If we canvassed the U.S. for other people who are millionaires, or well off, or financially comfortable, we'd find hundreds of thousands of them, almost all of whom got there by their own hard work.

To be fair, I suppose there must be a few people who became millionaires by thievery – but I don't know of any. But, you protest, the rich thief would keep his identity a secret, wouldn't he? Well, yeah. But that's part of it, too. Computer millionaires don't have to hide. Don't have to look over their shoulders. Don't have to worry about where or when to spend their money. Don't have to worry if they left a fingerprint somewhere or an image on a video camera. Don't have to worry about the name on their passport. Don't have to hide in some sleazy neighborhood and peek cautiously out the blinds every time a cop car goes by.

But thieves do have to do such things. People who work to earn their own money are able to be strong and confident and open and outgoing. Thieves are not.

Learning new things through your work adds to your life. There is no downside to learning something useful and new. Acquiring a computer by theft adds a small asset to your life – the computer – but also creates a negative in your life by subtracting a certain amount of comfort and ease from everyday living.

If I buy a computer and load it up with great software and peripherals, I can invite in everybody I know to show it off. If I steal a computer, I have to hide it – either physically or with camouflaging lies.

(And if I was writing this chapter about lies rather than about theft, right here I'd say "Damn, but lying is a lot of work!" If you habitually tell lies, you have to work very hard to remember what lies you've told, often invent other lies to defend them, and sometimes even make up completely new lies to get out of tight spots the first lies got you into. The real world, the world of facts, becomes your enemy. Whereas if you habitually tell the truth, there's nothing you particularly have to concentrate to remember, and the real world becomes an ally.)

I'd have to hide the computer, that is, unless I lived with other thieves. Except if I knew they were thieves there would probably be few of them I'd fully trust.

Living among thieves, you might trust the ones you know directly, but the ones you don't know directly, you can't trust. One of the great things about living among people who make a deliberate practice of honesty is that not only can you trust the ones you know personally, you can also more easily trust the ones you *don't* know.

A few years back, I worked at a company where there was an extremely high level of honesty. Unlike some other places I'd worked, I never even *heard* of anyone losing anything to theft. I probably knew less than 10 percent of my coworkers, but in seven years, I never had so much as a pencil missing off my desk.

I had coworkers who would leave billfolds or checkbooks on their desks while they went downstairs, or even out of the building, and nobody even thought about touching them. It was wonderfully relaxing working in a place like that – your desk was as safe as your home.

I've known a few thieves personally, and have been around a few more. There was nothing relaxing about them. A kid I knew in high school had the annoying habit, anytime we went out to eat or drink, of insisting that he had to sit so he could see the door. If other friends were already seated when we got there, often somebody had to move so he could sit in view of the door. I found out later it was because he didn't want to have his back turned when the police, or some of his many victims, came after him.

Then there was the sneaky little jerk who lived next door to me a few years back. The nephew of the woman who actually paid the rent, he seemed to spend a lot of his time sitting on the porch smoking cigarettes and sneering at the people who drove by, but he also had a series of furtive visitors, day and night. The whole thing looked fishy to me, but I gave him the benefit of the doubt and was always cordial to him – until the night I looked out and saw some of his friends coming out of my back shed with a couple of gas cans I kept there for lawn mower and chain saw fuel.

I didn't manage to catch them in the act, but I did find out where they lived. I made it clear to all of them that if I ever saw any of them anywhere near my house, I'd do everything in my power to see them in jail.

My sneaky neighbor abruptly moved out – he'd been living rent-free with his aunt – and I never saw him in the neighborhood again. I'm guessing he didn't dare come back.

He probably departed feeling he was somehow ahead of the game. He and his friends got a couple of gas cans and a few gallons of gas out of the deal.

The value of it, all told, might have amounted to about $35 worth of gas and cans. But the *price* of it was that he could never visit his aunt again, or come into the neighborhood, without fear of getting arrested. He lost his rent-free home, too. It seems to me that was some darned expensive gas.

Stealing weakens you directly, but it also weakens the society in which you live. The price of this theft, for instance, fell on others: Not only did I have to put up security lights and start locking my shed, everyone in the neighborhood probably became a wee bit less trusting of certain people, less inclined to give them the benefit of the doubt.

There's a feedback effect on the lot of us. Overall, as a result of theft and other predatory dishonesty, everybody has to labor just a little bit harder to make everything work.

Dumbing down

Does stealing make you less intelligent? Or is it that only less intelligent people fall into it?

A police officer I know, after several years on the force both as a patrol officer and a detective, once told me he thought most of the people who steal do it because they're so stupid they're almost unable to do anything else.

We have this myth that thieves are powerful, smart, got-it-together characters in full control of their lives as they prey on the weak. But the reality is that most of them are so incapable of making a living on their own they'd otherwise be on welfare.

Maybe they see themselves as predators, as lions ruling the savanna, but they're more like dopey, half-conscious little parasites – ticks stuck to the backsides of the *real* lions. All their lives, they have to have the blood and sweat of others to suck.

Stick them alone in the wilderness, or just alone in a small town with nobody to prey on, and they couldn't figure out where to find a steady meal if their lives depended on it.

And if you want to talk about weakness, other than an actual invalid, or somebody on his deathbed, there's probably no weaker person in society today than the convicted felon in prison. He's not allowed to decide on his own even when to eat. Even after he gets out, some significant part of his life is controlled by somebody else. Attempting to prey on others, in the end he stupidly traps himself into the weakest position of all.

Avoiding all that is pretty smart, seems to me.

Thou Shalt Not

So this has all been most illuminating, right? Hopefully you agree with me on some of these reasons it's bad to steal. And actually, I hope you have at least one new idea about the reasons for not stealing, something you hadn't thought of before, but that rings true to you.

Which brings me to this question: What part of "Thou Shalt Not Steal" could teach you any of this?

None of it.

One of the most vivid memories from my childhood days at Harvester's Tabernacle Baptist Church Sunday School was Sister Eldridge's face glaring fiercely into mine as she described how sinners – including liars and thieves – would be burned in a lake of fire, forever. Since I'd recently burned my hand touching a grill on the front of my grandmother's heater, and still had painful cross-hatched blisters on the tips of my fingers, I was scared out of my wits.

So I really paid attention to the lesson that if you stole something you were going to burn.

But long years later, I have no memory of Sister Eldridge talking about the good results of not stealing, or not lying. In fact, I can remember very little said in a positive vein on any ethical subject. It was only after I became an adult and started thinking about it on my own that I started to really appreciate all the good results of not stealing, not lying, not killing.

Alongside all that negative motivation, the "do not" lessons about stealing, where were the "do" lessons? Shouldn't there, in all such ethical training, be some positive motivation, all the reasons it's good to respect the property of others? Something about the happy side effects of not stealing? In place of the pure fear motivation to scare the childhood-you away from theft, shouldn't there always be equally emphatic pleasure motivation to draw you towards the reverse of it?

If there was, I never heard it in the Sunday School I went to.

It seems to me that exclusively negative lessons have some side effects – negative ones – of their own.

If all you have to motivate honesty is the intimidating, punitive stuff, if young people are honest only because they're filled with the fear of some horrifying punishment you've promised them, you create a condition that will result in plenty of them deliberately *choosing* to be dishonest.

Because we humans on our way to adulthood pass through a phase of aggressively challenging our personal fears (or meekly continuing to live with them), some number of us will decide "You'll be punished if you steal" means "You can steal ... if you're brave enough to dare the threats of punishment."

Dishonesty – lying, cheating, stealing – can actually become one of the ways to demonstrate courage.

Certainly, where I grew up, the theory got some support in the widely accepted example of "preacher's kids" – who were known to be considerably wilder than average. Perhaps more squashed down by preaching than the rest of us, because they had to live with it 24/7, they had to work harder to evoke the courage that let them discover their own adult individuality.

Swallowing the poison

Focusing on theft here might make you think I'm only talking about the effect stealing has on you, but the truth is, the principle holds for everything you do. Some things make you bigger and better and more appealing, some things make you smaller, weaker and less appealing. Lying, killing, cheating, bullying, rape – in addition to the effects on others which we all recognize, all those things also have a profound effect on *you*.

If you lie all the time, you become a habitual liar, a lifestyle and identification that has more than a few bad side effects. If you cheat constantly, you become a perpetual cheater. If you kill, you become a killer, and things are even worse.

All of which means: even if you "get away with it," you don't get away with it. You can't get away with it, even if nobody else ever finds out. Because everything is connected in your head, everything you do affects *you*. Changes you, turns you into something stronger and better, or something weaker and worse ... in some cases into something even you can't stand to live with.

It's not that some celestial power has decreed that bad things weaken you and good things make you stronger, it's that some acts weaken you, others make you stronger, and so that's how we *know* they are bad or good things. Stealing is a bad thing because it makes your victim *and you* worse off.

In the real world, it turns out, there are lots of reasons not to steal, or lie, or kill.

But they have nothing and less than nothing to do with heavens, hells, or gods.

HANK FOX

9

Good Without Gods

Okay, so why shouldn't you, especially if you're an atheist, just rob and rape and do whatever you please before you die? Why *really*?

Well ...

Let's say you go to the Pineview Baptist Church.

Picture an imaginary box that represents the church and its congregation, a container for all the practices, beliefs and acts the church holds dear.

Somewhere in this box is the subject and substance of Morality – all the actions, arguments, rationale and justification for being Good. Probably every member of PBC would tell you that Morality is wholly contained within the box of Pineview Baptist.

They'd say you couldn't have morality without being a member of their religion. Some of them might even say you couldn't be *really* moral without being a member of their specific church. To those people, no deliberate moral act could take place outside the Baptist Church, or, specifically, Pineview Baptist Church. "If there is no God, what keeps you from robbing and raping?" is really the speaker's way of saying just that.

Considering that we're talking about a mental model of the relationship between religion and morality, let's call that morality-contained-within-PBC idea Morality Model 1.

Can Model 1 be valid? Let's look at a moral issue for a moment and see if it holds up.

For now, we'll avoid hot-button subjects such as abortion and rape and sending your kids to Father Feely's Choirboy Training Ranch, and go for something small and non-controversial, a pastorally positive moral act: "Open doors for old people."

Do you have to be a member of PBC to know this moral point? Nope. A Baptist? Obviously not.

You only have to know it.

Which means, simply and instantly, that Model 1 is not the right one. Under even the simplest and most basic scrutiny, Model 1 doesn't hold up. Morality – at least as far as door opening is concerned – is not exclusively contained within Pineview Baptist Church.

If you thought goodness arrived only in a PBC wrapper, you'd never know it, though. You'd argue forever that morality was what *your* church said it was, and nothing else, and would focus on what your church wanted people to do rather than on good, fair, decent behavior. To you, every other approach would look like immorality ... while to the people in other churches, it might be *you* who looked immoral.

Note that insistence on the truth of Model 1 is not just a questionable idea that a few people hold from time to time. It is widespread and extremely persistent.

How about we consider a Morality Model 2? In Model 2, religion itself, some kind of devout faith, is the real deal, the true source of morality.

In this model, PBC exists within the larger framework of Religion – as, apparently, does Morality. This might not mean that any particular church in this larger box would necessarily contain morality. There might be churches that were decidedly immoral – say one where the leaders of the church forced old people to open the doors for them, because the leaders were considered the Chosen Ones.

But as long as they open doors for their elders, you could have Muslim moralists, Jewish moralists, Shinto moralists, even Judeo-Christian-Islamic Hootenanny moralists. But under Model 2, you could *not* have agnostic moralists. You could not have moralists who had never heard of religion. You could not have atheist moralists.

People really believe that. As an atheist, I've occasionally been confronted with the interesting argument "If you're a good person, you're really a Christian whether you know it or not." It makes me think some people could see a dog eat grass and conclude it must be a pony.

Does Model 2 hold water?

Certainly there are plenty of Muslims and Jews who open doors for old people. Probably even Shintoists and Zoroastrians and Wiccans do it.

But do agnostics ever open doors for old people? Do atheists?

Having been both, and having known a number of atheists and agnostics, I can tell you the answer to that: They do.

That has to mean either that agnostics and atheists are really Hootenanny church material without knowing it or that Model 2 also fails to hold up.

I know for a fact there are atheists and agnostics, lots of them, who walk around day after day and not only open doors for older people but also completely fail to rape or kill anyone. Likewise, there are some Christians – and devout members of other faith traditions – who walk around day after day with murder and rape in their hearts and on their hands.

In a turnaround of the earlier argument that a moral person, even an avowed atheist, must be a Christian without knowing it, some people would insist that even a lifelong churchgoer was not a "real" Christian if he was capable of thinking or doing such things. Yeah, and maybe a horse that bucks off its rider isn't a "real" horse.

Regardless, Model 2 also doesn't hold up. Morals do not come exclusively from membership in some major faith tradition.

Is there another mental model of morality, a Morality Model 3?

There is.

For Pineview Baptist Church members, it's this: Pineview

Baptist has no causal connection at all to Morality. Morals do not depend on the specific religious beliefs of Pineview members. Neither are Pineview members automatically moral.

Furthermore, for religious people in general, morality and religion-in-general have no causal connection. Morals do not depend on basic religious beliefs. Neither are religious people automatically moral.

Down at the real-world base, here's the real deal on morality: the box of Religion is totally separate from the box of Morality. Religion itself has no causal connection to morality. Immersing yourself in God, gods or holy books doesn't make you moral.

In fact, the *only* link between the two is the shaky one that religious people deliberately make in an attempt to make their religion seem necessary – the hijacking of morality by the members of Pineview Baptist Church, along with the pompous crowing that only they are blessed with a moral code.

On a side note, it's worth pointing out here that the Ten Commandments, which are often touted by fundamentalist Christians as some sort of ultimate moral anchor that simply *must* be shared with everyone, are not all that moral. The commandment to honor your mother and father is probably universally felt to be a good thing, but what can an outsider make of the commandments to "have no other gods before me" or to "remember the Sabbath and keep it holy"? Not only is there nothing in polite society that requires a person to remember the Sabbath, but remembering the Sabbath has nothing at all to do with helping create a polite society. These are sheer sectarian huckstering, as are one or two others –

depending on which Ten Commandments you're reading – and have no bearing at all on moral behavior in a culturally complex society.

If you're going to have only ten ultimate moral statements you hope to share with your entire society, it just seems a waste to devote three or four of them to home-church cheer-leading.

The fact that the boxes of Religion and Morality are separate does not mean that PBC members can't be extremely moral people. It does mean that moral people do not have to belong to PBC, or Judeo-Christian-Islamic Hootenanny, or any religion.

PBC members are not moral because they're PBC members. JCIH believers are not moral because they're JCIH believers. Neither are moral people somehow automatically PBC or JCIH members without knowing it.

People are moral because they care enough to make an effort to be good. Period.

Having said that morality does not come "exclusively" from PBC or some major faith tradition, it might seem that I leave the door open to churches as imperfect-but-acceptable places to learn morality. Some people think carefully selected churches are peachy-keen places to learn morals, and even agnostics sometimes send their kids to Sunday School to pick up the basics of "good" behavior.

However, there are some other problems with the traditional mental model of Religion Equals Morality. It turns out that both Model 1 and Model 2 have costs.

Simple Confusion

If morality consists of a body of good acts, it would be best if everybody knew just what those acts were, and how to do them. Right?

So:

Open Doors for Old People

There, how hard is that?

But if one group after another overlays that with a sectarian advertisement – which they do – will the core message get through? Or will it become a mere side issue to the more loudly-proclaimed sectarian point?

"Pineview Baptist Church invites you to worship with us this Sunday, when Pastor Jimmy Bob Phillips will offer a sermon on the subject "Why We Open Doors for Our Good Pineview Baptist Elders.""

"We Judeo-Christian-Islamic Hootenanists are the Chosen People Because We Are the Sole Possessors of the Holy Truth of Morality, Which is 'Open Doors for Old People.' Those With the Truth of JCIH in Their Souls Shall Ascend Upon Death to an Immortal Paradise, Where All the Doors Shall be Opened, and Nobody Shall Be Old, Ever, and Besides, if There *Are* Doors, They Shall Have Those Supermarket Electric Eye Thingies and Open on Their Own Anyway. Whereas All the Rest, the Wicked Non-Door-Openers, Shall Burn Forever in Locked Rooms, While Demons Fornicate With Them With Flaming Demon Weenies, and They Shall Cry Forever for the Doors to Open, But the DoorKeeper Shall Turn Away His Face and Hear Them Not. So Join JCIH or Burn Forever, Heathen Scum."

Churches, being churches, sometimes get quite wrong what moral behavior is. Those in the deep South were some of the strongest champions of slavery, and as recently as my own childhood, Southern Baptist churches were still aggressively segregated.

To some significant extent, churches often act as purveyors of sectarian rules rather than as champions of some larger moral code. Granted, churches serve as more than morality schools, but even non-churchy people often tend to see morality as a church issue. Religions have had a traditional lock on the subject of morality – so much so that in many places and times it has been practically forbidden to focus on the subject as a whole in any institution but a church.[12]

The problem is, presented with the rhetoric of PBC, and JCIH, and forty or fifty other churches, sects and "faith-based" groups, your average guy on the street is going to be considerably confused about just what constitutes good behavior. A young person might even conclude that if so many different groups disagree about this business of opening doors for old people, maybe it's not that good anyway. Maybe opening doors for old people is just sectarian bull poop. Maybe *all* of morality is sectarian bull poop. Worse, if he decides to give up his religion, maybe the package deal forces him to close the gate on trying to be caring, compassionate and law-abiding.

Wasted Resources

Imagine that you have a limited amount of time, energy and intelligence to bring to bear on a big problem – which is very much the case, isn't it? Some of the things on your To Do list never get done.

Now imagine that you spend half of your problem-solving time, energy and intelligence on solving the problem and the

---

12   Not to mention the fact that anytime you see a televised panel discussion on some aspect of morality, the panel will inevitably be dominated by people with divinity degrees.

other half on some other thing. That other thing might be interesting or fun or useful in some way, but it does nothing to solve the problem.

How quickly, efficiently and thoroughly will the problem get solved?

It makes sense that it will probably be solved less quickly, efficiently and thoroughly if you divert energy into other things than if you devote *all* of your time, energy and intelligence to the problem.

But then again, we're all only human. Maybe it's impossible to give a problem your all. Maybe you only have 50 percent of yourself you can bring to bear on a problem. Still, of that 50 percent, if you put 25 percent into the problem and the other 25 percent into dusting and genuflecting to your Our Lady of the Open Door shrine, how soon is the problem solved? It's obvious: Less quickly than if you had used your "whole" 50 percent of problem-solving ability.

If morality and religion are separate conceptual fields, separate boxes, and you have the goal of increasing moral behavior, but you try to do it by spending a large amount of your energy on the morality-and-religion-together Model 1 or 2, just how much good do you accomplish?

Considering that you and your group will expend some of their time and energy in chanting, speaking in tongues, handling snakes, adjusting your funny hats, kneeling and praying with Brother Pat, lighting candles, arranging incense, polishing up the gold elephant statues, cutting parts off babies, poring over bomb designs – whatever your particular religion demands you do – you will definitely have less time for door opening. You will get *less* accomplished with your limited time, energy and intelligence applied to the mixed effort than if you had focused the full of your available resources on moral behavior alone.

The sad fact is, if your main focus is your religion and not your morality, you and your friends become *less* able to achieve some full measure of morality.

Going the Wrong Way

When you have a possible answer to a serious problem, you don't just sit there. You take your answer and run with it. You make some effort, you spend money, you travel far down the road to where you think the answer lies, in an attempt to solve that problem.

So if what you have is a *wrong* answer, by the time you realize your mistake, if ever, you have already expended money, time and effort on it. In the case of bad directions to get somewhere, for instance, you may have gone quite some physical distance in the wrong direction.

That means you don't just stop being wrong in one instant and start being right in the next. Oh, no. First, you have to fix the wrong part. You have to *give up on* the money you've lost, you have to *accept as lost* the effort you've expended. You have to actively *turn around and go back* over the misguided distance you've traveled. You have to spend even more money, time and effort to get back on track.

Regarding morality and religions, that means that if you have a wrong answer about moral behavior, you just can't instantly and easily fix it. A price has to be paid.

The first part of that price, the part where you have to admit you're wrong and consciously accept that you've wasted some significant part of your time and life, and have an uphill slog ahead of you to get back to zero ... for some people, that alone is too much to undertake.

In human terms, movement has a psychological momentum as well as a physical one. I couldn't guess how many times I've been a mere hundred feet from my door when I realized I'd forgotten something, and automatically decided not to go back for it because it was "too much trouble."

Words from On High

Finally, and importantly, if you believe that morals are handed down by mystical superbeings rather than worked out among rational, compassionate adults, you will never really "get" morality.

It is impossible to be a moral being yourself, or a positive moral force in your society if you don't understand something of the *reasons* for moral acts. People who think that only religious faith keeps you from committing crimes – and I've heard that silly question often enough "If you don't believe in God, what keeps you from committing murder anytime you feel like it?" that it must be a pretty common idea – have no way to think about morality beyond "I have to do what my god says."

Worse, contained within that question, a question suggested by everything taught in churches, is the statement that the natural desire of human beings is to rob and kill others and the only thing restraining them is their good Christian faith. Freighted within the question is the clear implication that compassion, love, charity, tenderness and decency are unnatural, alien traits to humans, and become available *only* after you start to believe in God. For people who believe that, every person outside their religion is automatically wicked.

To me, this is so far beyond insulting – not just to me but to the entire human species – it's just plain filth.

Knowing nothing of the nature of morality, such a person might live his entire life blindly following rules handed down to him by others. Those rules might be anything from "Open doors for old people" to – I kid you not – "Beat your wife to death if she allows another man to see her bare face." He would neither be able to teach an adequate moral code to others nor be able to respond to some new situation requiring on-the-spot moral judgment.

He would never ask himself what's good about being good. He would never be able to understand that people with different beliefs can be every bit as good as he is.

For instance, why open doors for old people? Why *really*?

Because it's good to help those less strong than ourselves – it costs you almost nothing but might mean a great deal to the person you do it for.

Because it's a win-win: It gives you a good feeling to know you're helping someone, and it gives them a good feeling that someone cares enough to offer help.

Because if you help maintain the tradition of young people opening doors for elders, you yourself will probably someday benefit.

Because generous acts help maintain an overall friendly atmosphere in your society, which benefits everybody. If you help some elderly person, it's likely someone else will follow your example and help your own parents or grandparents ... or your pregnant wife, or a handicapped child, or just someone tired and harried and in need of a little human caring.

Because compassion feels good, and even though the beneficiary of the act may be a total stranger, the act itself makes you a better person for yourself and your family.

Compare this list of *reasons* to the juvenile, simplistic "Because my supernatural sky-daddy commands it." The two mindsets are not even in the same ballpark.

The same process holds for every other aspect of morality.

Why not rob and rape? For good *reasons*, and not because Jehovah commands it.

Why not simply kill people who annoy you? For good *reasons*, and not because of red letters in the Bible.

Why help the less fortunate? For good *reasons*, and not because Allah looks down and approves.

The guy who understands the real mechanics of morality is far more advanced, morally, than someone who robotically does what he's commanded, who fearfully does "good" acts to avoid eternal fire, or who selfishly chalks up goodie points only for the purpose of bargaining for his own everlasting life.

He's also a much better neighbor to those who hold other faiths, or no faith at all.

HANK FOX

The Price of Faith

HANK FOX

10

Sucking Up to the Virgin Mary

I see these press releases from churches every week in the newspaper. One of them in particular caught my eye.

A little shrine near where I live was having a special Adoration of the Virgin Mary event, and the description of it included a "procession in praise of the Sacred Virgin Mary," followed by a sermon on the virtues of the Sacred Virgin Mary and ending with an elaborate ceremony in praise of that very same Sacred Virgin Mary.

I had to chuckle. Wow, that was an awful lot of praising of the Sacred Virgin Mary in one little press release. And wow, that was going to be an awful lot of sucking up to the Sacred Virgin Mary in one little event.

Really, does the Sacred Virgin Mary really *need* all that

earnest fawning bestowed upon her?

I mean, I can imagine people during medieval times thinking they had to bow and scrape like this in the presence of a queen or prince – and the Royal Person actually expecting and needing it – but there's something comically unclean about the thought of real people doing it today.

And yet these people are deadly serious about it.

There's a whole long speech I could get into here about the inner nature of people desperate for praise and adulation, the basic idea of which is that nobody truly big and powerful would need or want such toadying.

Anybody who knows the basics of how people work inside could tell you that the person who demands constant praise from others has desperately low self-esteem. Being unable to feel good about himself on his own makes him a sort of addict – he needs a frequent fix of "feel-good" from others because he's unable to generate it on his own.

On the other hand, it seems to me that a guy (or even a Sacred Virgin) who really didn't need it would be sickened by all the wheedling, flattery and devotion. I start to see the scene as something like a Monty Python skit, with the lot of them dancing around and singing a demented ditty:

> O, you Virgin Mary, you are so very nice.
> We shower you with praises, we shower you with rice.
> We tell you we adore you, we tell you that you're swell.
> We really, really like you – please don't send us to Hell.

But I won't go into that whole long speech because a really terrible realization came to me shortly after I read the notice about the event, a cascade of thoughts that went something like this:

Imagine the work that went into this one event.

Total up all the labor of the people to arrange and advertise it.

Add in the efforts of all the people who would come and be part of it – all the showering, shaving and dressing, all the shepherding of kids and great aunts, all the tying-up of dogs, the bringing-in of cats, the fueling of cars, the packing of baby things, all the time and money spent traveling to and from.

Go back and add in all the work that went into building this one tiny shrine, and maintaining and using it over the decades – the building, dedicating, cleaning, publicizing, volunteering, painting, wiring, amping, repairing, carving, grass cutting, landscaping, stained-glass-window making, stained-glass-window cleaning, sign-making, remodeling, refurbishing, preaching, kneeling, breast pounding, head thumping, and hosanna singing.

And then multiply that by, oh, ten million or so, to include all the effort devoted to all the services in all the churches in all the world, in all of human history and pre-history. Multiply that by a factor of two or three or ten to calculate in all the thought and effort and worry and fear that went into such goddy pursuits in people's spare time.

Now gather all that human sweat and devotion and creativity and imagination and worry and concern in one big ball and imagine what could have been done with it.

You know those ancestors of ours from 20,000 years or so ago? No, not the Neanderthals – the other ones. The Cro-Magnons, the "modern" humans.

It's hard for me to believe those people were stupid. They even had bigger brains than we do. I suspect they were every bit as smart as you and I, and considering that they didn't have the cushion of civilization, they may even have been smarter than either of us. Possibly even *much* smarter.

Maybe they had to be. Whereas our dullards today are cradled in a supportive society, their dullards were eaten by saber-toothed tigers or stomped to death by woolly mammoths.

Snatch a Cro-Mag kid out of the past and drop him into a modern kindergarten and he'd probably do just fine, school-wise. He might do better than fine – give him a little caring and encouragement and he might be one of those kids who go to college at the age of 12 and end up with a Ph.D. by the time they're 15.

Think about all that brainpower back there in the distant past.

And then think about the very brief span of modern history from the first stirrings of organized and directed capital-S Science[13] to the time when men walked on the moon. It really took only three or four hundred years.

What the hell happened to us?

Renaissance Italians could have had genetic engineering.

The Greeks could have had a real science of the human mind.

The Egyptians could have had a space program.

If we'd started 20,000 years ago, those of us alive today could have been functional immortals living on a paradise planet, with no population problems, no pollution, and no energy

---

13   *Arbitrarily, I date it from the founding of the Royal Society in the 1600s.*

shortages.

Hell, we could be conversing with genetically-engineered English-speaking elephants by now, watching book-writing chimpanzees being interviewed on Mars by Oprah.

Instead ... we're here. Only *here*.

We have people – real, actual human beings, somebody's mommy and daddy, and somebody's favorite little girl – *dying* because we can't seem to get enough food to everybody. Dying because we're too stupid to understand the limits to reproduction in an environment with limited resources.

We have coral reefs dying all over the world. Oceans being fished out. Elephants killed for farmland. Chimpanzees and gorillas shot to death for *meat*. Whales slaughtered for sushi. Bulls and bears and dogs tortured and killed for entertainment.

And we have wars and wars and more wars. As I write this, even my own nation is involved simultaneously in two major ones.

What happened to us? I'm suddenly afraid I know...

What if all that effort we talked about earlier, all that building, dedicating, cleaning, publicizing, volunteering, painting, wiring, amping, repairing, carving, grass cutting, landscaping, stained-glass-window-making, stained-glass-window-cleaning, sign-making, remodeling, refurbishing, preaching, kneeling, breast pounding, head thumping, and hosanna singing ...

Well, what if *that* was what took place instead of all the possible inventing, researching, thinking, planning, building, feeding, imagineering, engineering, launching, exploring, questing, loving, preserving, protecting, creating and curing?

What if the past 20,000 years was, instead of twenty millennia of boundless human discovery and progress and understanding …

What if it was just 20,000 years of wasted time? What if it was 20,000 years of mental illness? Religious intoxication? Mystical masturbation?

What if we spent the whole time, most of us, singing our drunken hosannas in nervous determination, smiling with forced unconcern as the possibilities of greatness passed us by?

For generations. For millennia.

What if that was the case?

Well, if it was, and it seems to me all too believable that it might have been, then it would be really, really terrible.

It would be a tragedy off the scale of anything I can imagine.

11

Deadline Pressure

Wh
hat would you do if you only had one day to see, before having an operation that would save your life but render you blind for the rest of it?

Me? I'd get up early and watch the sunrise over the mountains.

I'd go to the zoo and look into the eyes of a tiger.

I'd visit my friend's backyard bird feeding station and stare at blue jays and cardinals until I'd burned their brilliant blues and vibrant reds into my memory.

I'd gather together everybody I'd ever loved and spend hours just looking at their faces.

I'd gaze down into a lake and watch clouds float past in the reflected sky.

I'd go to a park and watch children playing.

I'd drive to a museum and spend an hour or so looking at classic paintings.

I'd take a walk on the beach and savor the last sunset I'd ever see.

I'd stay up late watching the stars, hoping to see one last brilliant slash of a meteor across the darkness.

And then I'd go dancing until dawn and watch people moving together in love and celebration.

Now let me ask you this: When's the last time you had a day that was anything like this?

Never, right?

But then again, you're not going to wake up blind tomorrow morning, are you? You've got a long, long time to get everything done.

There's no pressure. No deadline.

And if you believe in an afterlife, it's even less pressing. On some level, you really do think you have forever.

And therein lies a problem.

The things you really believe really do have a powerful effect on your actions. In fact, I'll go so far as to say that it is *impossible* to strongly believe a thing and not have it affect all that you think and do.

And all of us know it. If you believe you have 24 hours to do a book report, chances are you're reading the book right now. If you believe you have six weeks to do that book report, it's a good bet that you haven't even been to the library yet.

If you really and truly believe in an afterlife, the deadline pressure for everything is zero. You will go through your entire life believing in second chances, happy endings in some distant better place, and it will affect how you live your life and how you deal with others.

To add a bit of personal perspective on the subject of deadline pressure, let me change tracks for a bit:

Loggers in paradise

I stood once in a little museum on the south shore of Lake Tahoe, inspecting a photo of loggers taken in the year 1860 or so.

The Virginia City silver mines were booming at the time, and their voracious appetite for shoring timbers were satisfied from the shores of nearby Lake Tahoe.

The huge ponderosa pines of that era would have been breathtaking to those of us alive today, who think "tree" means something you can walk up to and put your arms around. This photo was of one of those felled giants, with a couple of dozen loggers posed before and atop it. A team of mules stood to the side, and a loose dog had wandered into the shot.

"Smile for the camera" was unknown in those days, and the miners in the picture simply stand and stare at you from that distant sunny day, more than 54,000 days in the past.

For me, it was one of those accidental moments that brand themselves onto your brain and stay with you forever. This was the first time in my life that I looked at a historical photo and understood that the people pictured had actually lived.

These two dozen men were people, real living people, a lot like me.

Can you imagine them as real? As real in their time as you and I are right now?

They had friendships, pains and sorrows, they laughed out loud, they gazed out over the lake in quiet moments, they woke up some mornings thinking "Oh, my head! What did I *do* last night?"

They worked and played and wrote letters home. They got sick and got well, bled and healed, cursed and shouted in anger, fought and made peace, carried grudges, shared coffee and lies and cheap whiskey with logging partners around the campfire. Their lives held feelings and meaning, soaring dreams and crushing frustrations, vast satisfactions and shortchanged futilities.

This guy was the rough-mannered foreman of the camp. And that one coveted his job. This one over here wanted to make enough money to go back and marry his childhood sweetheart. This other one came west to forget his childhood sweetheart. This one was a father, this one his son. That one there played the banjo before he lost two fingers in an accident. This one was straitlaced, this one obscene, this one generous, this one mean.

Some died young, maybe only days after this photo was taken. Some lived to ripe old ages. Some of them married later and had kids, and told them stories of the days when they cut wood on the shores of a beautiful crystal clear lake.

But sooner or later, they all died.

Every one of them had biographies, if you were to write them, every bit as long and complex as mine and yours. They lived whole lives, birth to death and everything in between, and did all the different kinds of things that humans do. But now their entire histories were silenced.

Lost.

Over.

Nobody even knows their names. Nothing remains of them but this modern reproduction of an aged photo – old silver crystals on crumbling yellowed paper. All there is left of them is an echo of an echo of one frozen second of their lives.

This was the thought that slammed into me as I stood looking at that photo:

Everybody in this picture, and *everybody who ever knew them*, is now ... gone.

It was a shocking realization. An epiphany. A real corker.

And here's today's corker:

Look around you. Look at the people you love. Look at your job. Look at your car and your house. Look at your childhood sweetheart, and your kids, and your friends and neighbors.

Everybody you know, and everybody who knows them – everybody who knows *you* – is, in some not-so-distant future, just as dead and gone.

Nobody even knows your name. Unless you're Abraham Lincoln or somebody equally history-worthy, nothing you did left a sign.

From that future day, your whole life is lost in some distant past. All your feelings and meaning, your soaring dreams and crushing frustrations, your vast satisfactions and shortchanged futilities, all amount to less than a grain of sand on an endless beach.

You're gone.

Over.

Lost.

This is about the crappiest, scariest idea you could ever have forced on you. Even if you know it's true, some large part of your backmind is right this second deliberately disbelieving it. It's just too shocking to think about.

It's probably the single biggest reason why most humans have some kind of religion. Even knowing about the billions of years in each direction from our lives, and even knowing about the vast and limitless space in all directions, some part of us has to think the whole universe is all about US. We want to be noticed. We want it all to mean something. More than that, we want it to mean something WE can understand. And we want it to go on meaning something.

But it doesn't go on.

It ends.

Everything those loggers failed to do in their lives, it ... Never. Got. Done.

They're not up there floating around in some logger heaven, admiring ghostly redwood trees or enjoying celestial dance hall girls.

From that future-day viewpoint, neither are you. Everything you failed to do likewise never got done.

All the times you passed up seeing the sunset, all the clouds you never looked up at, all the hundreds of times you might have said "I love you" to your wife, or husband, or grandmother, or child, or good friend, it never got done. All the adventures you didn't do, the rafting trip down the Grand Canyon, the cruise to Alaska, the sailing off to the Caribbean, the asking Betty Sue to the prom, all of that stuff, all of it, never got done.

Unless ... unless you've done it already. Unless you're doing it now. Unless you've got it on your schedule and are absolutely going to do it soon.

Death is the ultimate deadline pressure, the ultimate arbiter of what your life meant and what you accomplished.

The word "deadline" even says "dead" right in it. And it says "dead" because that's the absolute end point of the possibilities of getting a thing done in your life.

Slaves in church

I've thought many times that Christianity is just about the perfect religion for slaves.

Southern blacks lived out entire generations of involuntary servitude, and they did it, many of them, all the while dreaming of the happier, heavenly times to come.

After a lifetime of sweating in cotton fields, having your children sold away from you, being forced to submit to plantation owners' horny sons, after beatings, whippings, harsh words, after decades of servitude and mean conditions under the unmindful hands of people who never even saw you as humans, much less as humans with feelings, and then death in a squalid, cold shack ...

What could be more wonderful than to be told you would rise up to Glory, where St. Peter would cast off your slave shackles and welcome you into that bright warm place of eternal freedom and joy?

Yeah, right.

What more ugly trick could you play on slaves? I mean, aside from taking their freedom away and treating them like livestock for decades, how could you possibly make it worse?

You could make it worse by making them think it was

meant to be that way and that everything would work out just fine ... not *in* the end, but *after* the end.

All this good stuff would happen *only* if they were humble and meek while alive, submitting willingly to the life the Almighty God had ordained for them.

You'd make them think that not only was there no deadline pressure but that the reverse was true – that they would lose out if they did anything *before* the deadline.[14]

So that rather than going after everything they cared about, freedom and self-determination and accomplishments of their own, everything they might want in their lives and for their lives, they'd *wait*. Most of them wouldn't try to accomplish any of it – wouldn't even rebel from their slavery – but would sit meekly and quietly and do nothing for the whole of their lifetimes.

And the one thing that might possibly be worse than doing this to slaves would be this:

Doing it to yourself.

Voluntarily.

Having a whole world in which to adventure and learn and accomplish, and instead staying home and meekly accepting the crumbs of life. Falling into the mistake of believing a slave religion and letting it rule your personal world.

Thinking that you had forever and waiting until there was no time at all. Ignoring the deadline pressure because you didn't believe in the deadline.

Missing out on the Grand Adventure because you'd swallowed the Grand Lie.

---

14   *Certainly checking out voluntarily via suicide would be the wickedest of sins. And what do you know? It IS.*

12

Reading & Reason

Years ago, I was driving from Texas to California, and I picked up this hitchhiker.

Yeah, yeah, I know – it's dangerous to pick up hitchhikers. But it was a different time back then, and I had a good sense about these things. This young man was harmless.

Anyway, here we were, riding along in my pickup, talking about this and that, and I happened to read one of the road signs out loud: "Arizona, 58 miles."

The fellow digested that for a few moments and then asked "Is Arizona a town? Or a *state*?"

For a moment, I was so surprised I couldn't think of what to say. I mean, the guy was of at least average intelligence, and his accent clearly said he was an American; how could he not know that? – but I finally managed a calm answer.

He asked a couple of other odd questions in the hours we traveled together, questions that showed astounding gaps in basic knowledge, stuff available to, well, probably any third grader.

After fiddling around with the question for a bit, I came up with this daring idea: The guy couldn't read. The vast body of background knowledge in my head, so much stuff I took totally for granted, stuff I'd expect everybody would know by the time they were 12, this guy didn't seem to have the full dose.

Some of that stuff you get from talking to people or listening to them talk – like the rules of baseball or boxing. Some of it you get in school – like what happened at the Alamo, or what a hypotenuse is. Some of it you get from watching TV or movies, like who's buried in Grant's Tomb or how to use a shoulder-fired missile to bring down an enemy helicopter.

But some of it you'd only get from newspapers or magazines, books or web browsing. From reading.

I steered the conversation onto books. We'd been talking about the space program, and I began to tell him about a science fiction novel I'd just read. "You ever read any SF?" I asked.

"What's SF?" he returned.

"Science fiction. Time travel, that sort of stuff."

He looked away, out the window. "Naw. I don't read. I couldn't never learn how."

I've replayed his answer in my head any number of times since then, marveling at it in fresh horror.

I mean, hey, you see somebody in a wheelchair, you politely

open doors for them, give ground in supermarket aisles, that sort of thing. We set up special parking spaces for them – all of society recognizes that it's good to accommodate the needs of people in wheelchairs.

But for a guy who can't read, there's no kind of wheelchair. Even Braille won't help.

It's a damned shame, all around. A damned shame.

But ...

It ain't the worst shame.

There are these people who don't read because they just can't. And that's no fault of their own.

There are other people who don't read because they're not good at it. Maybe they had a bad experience in school and they have an aversion to books as a result. And that's bad, but also not totally their fault.

There's a third group of people who don't read ... well, because they're just too lazy. Or maybe just too busy. And that's their fault, and it's not good.

But there's this fourth group, and they deliberately don't read. Not that they can't. They won't. Purposefully, with something akin to jaw-clenched malice, these people choose not to read.

Excuse me, but that's just creepy.

Being too lazy to read is kind of like an infraction – the equivalent of driving 35 in a school zone or pumping up some bass-heavy music at 3 a.m.

Refusing to read, though, is a crime of violence. It's like mugging a man on the street who turns out to be your own self.

How can I explain the magnitude of the tragedy created by

someone who deliberately refuses to read?

Imagine that there's this huge banquet, just acres of delicious and interesting food, all spread out before you – and yet some people just totally turn their noses up at it. "No, I'll just have my grilled cheese sandwich, thank you."

Or there's this free world cruise, departing every hour, and it goes to 50 different ports, and you see dolphins and whales and stunning sunsets every day of the voyage. And some people just say "No, I think I'll just stay here on Smith Avenue. If it's farther than the corner store, I don't need it."

Refusing to read is like living in a country that provides free education to your kids, but you say "No, I'm not sending them to that school. I can't be bothered to make those darned lunches every day."

Reading is a gateway into a huge and interesting world, things you never knew you never knew, things both useful and mind-expanding. To think there are people who simply don't want any part of it is … baffling.[15]

I could understand it if I was really talking about an ocean cruise, or a huge banquet, or an exclusive private school. Some people get seasick, after all, or are allergic to stuff, or have anti-elitist feelings.

And lots of people just can't afford them. But *this* cruise ship, *this* vast buffet, *this* school, is all *free*! We have libraries in every city and town in the U.S., and it costs absolutely nothing to walk into one.

Thanks to libraries, reading is all smooth sailing, and hypo-

---

15   Yes, I'm aware that reading is not the only way to get information about the world. The difference between reading and something like TV, though, is that one of them allows you yourself to decide what sort of information you'll be taking in, the other puts some of the decisions in the hands of distant corporations, and charges you the extra price of forcing you to watch commercials.

allergenic, and as to elitism, free access to books is practically the keystone of equality.

Free knowledge is about the most leveling social force I can imagine on this earth.

Because reading lifts you up from wherever you are and makes you bigger and better.

There are books in libraries that tell you how to become a millionaire. Books that teach you every subject you can imagine – math and cake decorating and how to reroof your house. Books that make you laugh, books that make you cry. Books that lend you adventures. Books that show you how to be healthier, to live a longer and happier life. Books that invite you to step into the skin of distant others, letting you be anyone, anywhere, any*when* you want to be. Books that connect you with other people, making you a better citizen and neighbor, by helping you understand the strangers a thousand miles away, or the strangers next door.

And yet, it's still somehow true …

Some people don't want it.

Worst of all, some of these people not only don't want it for themselves, they don't want it for anyone. Not their kids, not your kids, not anybody.

The ones I'm talking about have slammed the door on every bright and noble future they might aspire to, have severed the link with all that they could be, and have chosen to remain what they merely are. They huddle within themselves, frightened and defensive, and they are absolutely unreachable by any word or thought or concept that is not already in their heads.

And they want everybody to be like them.

And the really weird thing is, all the people I've ever even heard of who are like this appear to be that way because of their religion. These are the fundamentalists, the ultra-conservatives. The anti-social, incurious religious luddites.

Given any specific subject, they depend on *one* book for their answers, a "holy" book written thousands of years ago[16], rather than the many more recent books on the subject written by experts with all the latest facts.

These are the people on that weird tiny slice of the social pie chart who think they have the One Truth, and everybody else and everything else is not just wrong but wicked.

They themselves don't read, and I suppose that would be tolerable if they stopped there. But since books are full of new ideas, new thoughts, strange new concepts, they don't want anyone else to read them, either. They don't want people to have free and uncontrolled access to uncensored, unedited, unapproved words.

They want Harry Potter off the shelves, and "The Age of Reason." They want "Brave New World" gone, and "The Call of the Wild." They object to "The Lorax" and "Dr. Zhivago." They want "1984" and "Fahrenheit 451" to go up in flames.[17] They devote time to attacking "The DaVinci Code." To say nothing of how they feel about books on sex, or evolution.

To them, all that adventure, all that knowledge, all that freedom of thought is somehow Evil.

I don't even have words to describe how strange, how sick, how un-American that seems to me.

---

16 *Except that many of them haven't even read it.*
17 *To which I say: The darkest shadows are those cast by the light of burning books.*

13

The Mob

I've always been curious about mobs.

I mean, you read about a fire in a nightclub, and more people die from being crushed to death in the exits than from the fire. Or a large group gathered on a bridge in the Middle East takes a sudden scare, and the next thing you know, hundreds are dead in a stampede. Or a soccer crowd furious at the result of the game storms onto the field and attempts to kill the players of the opposing team, with the result that a dozen bystanders die in the melee.

A stampede of humans. It just seems so ... odd.

I've worked with horses and cattle, and I can relate to the idea of a mass of animals fleeing in fear, with the fear feeding on itself, building, until nothing could stop it but the victims' exhaustion.

And I do understand that all of us critters have the same instincts to flee from danger, or sometimes to attack threats. I have a pretty good grasp of how panic in a group of animals can be passed on and amplified. If you're a cow in the middle of the herd, you might not even know about the nearby mountain lion; you run in bawling fear only because you see the white-eyed, foaming panic of the cows around you, the other cows see your panic and that makes them further afraid, and so on. None of you might have any idea what you're afraid of – you're only reacting to, and helping amplify, the fear around you.

But ... humans?

You have to wonder: If *I* were in a mass fear situation like this, would I turn into a panic-stricken animal and just join in with the shrieking, shoving, child-trampling mass?

I have no idea. Of course, like you reading this, I like to think I'd look around, find a still spot somewhere to see what was happening, and ride out the panic in safety, hopefully without killing others with my stomping feet.

I hope I'm already prone to not be part of a panic-stricken mob, or an enraged mob, mostly because I'd never be in the center of a crowd to begin with, but also because I have a relentless Guardian Worrywart that looks ahead and warns me of possible dangers (and even impossible ones) and looks for safety options.

And maybe, just maybe, having put some thought into mob action will inoculate me a bit, so I'll be less likely to instantly give up my conscious mind and pitch in with the next mob I happen to encounter.

You never know.

So what the heck *is* a mob? At first glance, it looks like it's a large group of people acting in highly emotional concert – responding to fear or rage, they flee or attack, and death and destruction ensues in minutes.

But what if mobs aren't just about uncontrolled fear or fury, and what if they don't only happen in very short periods of time and all in one place?

We all get some (possibly most, and for some people all) of our motivation from the people around us. Fads and fashions, attitudes and advertising jingles, catchy trends and cool slang sweep through populations in continuous waves. I buy a black shirt, you buy a black shirt, she buys a black shirt, and before you know it, we've started a subculture.

You can even see the effects in mass media. All of a sudden, you notice the news is all about plane crashes. Or it seems there's suddenly nothing on but stories of child abductions. All eyes turn to day care centers as a wild rash of physical abuse stories blanket the airwaves, or the viewing public apparently just can't get enough of Catholic priests fiddling around with altar boys.

These are slower and more diffuse versions of the same type of feedback loop that happens in a mob, but since most of it is relatively benign, it probably doesn't qualify as true mob action. Very few people die from outbreaks of fashion.

But to get a mob, I don't think you have to have angry villagers with pitchforks and torches storming a castle. You probably don't have to have someone scream "Fire!" in a crowded nightclub. And as I said before, it doesn't have to happen in minutes.

But it does seem that you have to have the sparks of fear, or the smell of rage, percolating through a crowd. Higher brain activity has to shut down, the mob-motive has to feed back on itself and amplify it until it's all-consuming, and the group has to become completely controlled by it.

Which leads me to an interesting conceptual leap:

Religious fundamentalism is a mob in slow motion.

Think about it.

There's the fear. Of death, or burning in hell, or homosexuals, or maybe just of being tempted into myriad "sins" by less devout neighbors.

There's anger, which plays out as a dislike – or even active hatred – of everybody who isn't a member of that particular sect, and everything they do, everything they enjoy, that the sect considers ungodly.

And there's the feedback aspect: I get the very strong impression that most fundamentalists listen to nothing but fundie-radio, watch nothing but fundie-TV, read nothing (if they read) but their holy book (approved version only, of course) or possibly fundie-approved books and magazines.

Then there's the higher-brain shutdown. Ever try to talk to a serious fundamentalist? It's surreal. It's like the two of you are speaking two totally different languages that by complete accident happen to use the same word-sounds. None of the words you use have the same meanings to them, and vice versa.

You say "true" and mean something like "factually-correct information," but they hear "mystical revelation by ancient holy man." You say "theory" with the strict evidential support of science in mind, and they hear something like "wild, unsupported conjecture meant to subvert the minds of God's chosen ones." You say "secular" and they hear "evil plot to destroy everything that's good."

And – in my experience – not only do they not understand you, they literally can't allow you to explain. Their minds aren't just closed, they're barricaded as if the Mongol hordes are coming to rape and murder everything they hold dear.[18]

Finally, there's the aspect of people getting hurt.

Fundamentalists don't just sit quietly at home and try to live by their own codes of ethics and dress and whatnot. Oh, no. They take to the streets. They pack school board meetings. They take out ads. They preach on billboards. They have TV shows. They blanket the radio waves 24/7. They build large organizations and collect huge sums of money.

They want *everybody* to adhere to their code. If they see something they don't like, they *shriek*.

They want you to act and dress as they act and dress. They want your kids to have access to no other books but the ones they approve. They want you to do this, and *not* do that (for instance, they want you to have sex *only* within their guidelines), and they're willing to brand you as evil and possibly even worthy of death for not doing it the "right" way.

---

18   Seriously, try sometime to explain to a fundamentalist that the word 'theory' has a technical definition different from the colloquial one. You'll get absolute, blank incomprehension. My own efforts have included a little argument about the word 'strike.' I say "The word 'strike' has one meaning if you're a bowler, a totally different meaning to a baseball fan, still another meaning to a union member, and even a fourth meaning to a drill-rig crew exploring for oil. If you're talking about baseball, or bowling, you have to use the meaning appropriate to that subject, right? You can't sit at a baseball game and yell 'Hey, that wasn't a strike! He didn't even knock down all the pins!' " Everything's fine until I say "The word 'theory' means one thing in everyday conversation, but it means something totally different when you're talking about a field of science, and that meaning is NOT 'a wild idea that just popped into my head.' " Every time, and I mean EVERY time I've advanced this argument, I've gotten in return the equivalent of "Nuh-uh! A 'theory' is a guess!" A few unusually obtuse opponents have even followed up with "You're trying to trick me!"

Fundamentalists don't just accidentally stomp people as they run here and there. They do it in slow motion, sometimes with full, eager, apparently conscious intent. They automatically think in terms of force, of hellfire and death penalties, when met with resistance.

We don't generally see fundamentalism in the West as extremely dangerous, but that's probably only because we have social and legal limits on how blatantly they're allowed to act out their "beliefs."

The idea of letting little girls die in a blazing building because they didn't have their heads covered,[19] and thus couldn't be allowed to come out where men might see them, seems distant and unlikely to us. Stoning a woman to death for allowing a man on the street to see her bare arm is a bit hard to swallow.

They can't get away with such things here and now.

But not only does it happen right now elsewhere in the world, things very like it happened here, and not that long ago.

The chilling part is that it could happen again, and fairly quickly, if our hometown fundamentalists had a free hand in running things.

The even more chilling part is that they're already trying.

Fundamentalism is a mob in slow motion.

And unless someone – you? – helps head them off, they just might someday turn up in a school board, city council, county board, state capital, or even White House, near you.

---

19 *It happened in Saudi Arabia in March 2002. The local Islamic decency police prevented a number of girls from escaping a burning building because their heads weren't properly covered. Fifteen died.*

14

The Downhill Road

Here's a Wise Old Saying for you:

Everything Good Is Uphill

But is it true? I took the mule ride to the bottom of the Grand Canyon a few years back. Halfway down, we came to the Indian Gardens rest stop, and there alongside the trail was an enormous patch of delicious, ripe blackberries.

So they were downhill, right? And since ripe blackberries are good, the saying has to be false.

But then again, considering that it took no small amount of fearful effort for me to ride a mule for several hours on this rocky, steep, breathtakingly dangerous trail – in some places, there are literally 500-foot drops off the edge of a three-foot-wide-and-no-guard-rail path – those good berries were, metaphorically speaking, far uphill.

"Uphill," in this case, doesn't mean literal uphill. It means "costing considerable effort." In the same sense, "downhill" means "requiring little or no effort."

To say it another way: It takes work to make good things happen.

If you're dropped into the top of a tree by a tornado, it doesn't take any effort on your part. You might scream and thrash in the powerful winds, expending a lot of energy, but none of it would be aimed specifically at the goal of getting to the top of the tree. You could be unconscious and limp as a corpse and still get there. Reaching the top of a tree via tornado, then, is a downhill thing.

On the other hand, to reach safety on the ground afterward, you'd definitely have to work at it. Trembling, heart pounding, carefully picking your way from limb to limb so you don't fall and die, you'd expend a considerable amount of energy and care. So climbing *down* the tree to safety would be uphill.

Don't think "uphill" only applies to muscular effort. Anybody who's ever asked someone out for a date for the first time knows how uphill it is, how much courage it can take. If you're 8 years old and standing in the doorway of a haunted house full of witches, skeletons and mechanical spiders lurching out at you from the darkness, overcoming the fear and going inside is definitely uphill.

So everything good is uphill. Valuable things are valuable because it takes work to get them. Even if we often forget it, we seem to be wired to know this.

So what's uphill? A college degree. A career. A remodeled house. A savings account. A trim, fit body. A head full of useful facts in a field you enjoy. The girl/guy of your dreams finally in your life. A clean car. A long hike. The ultimate vacation. A collection of really good photographs. Skill with an airbrush. A bowling trophy. A strong, supportive family. The entire collection of Spider-Man comics. The knowledge that you challenged and defeated your fears of that haunted house.

None of those good things happens by accident. They all take work, and lots of it. There is a strong, direct connection between effort and value.

Yes, some people win millions in the lottery. Completely worthless heiresses sometimes inherit vast wealth. But out of every million people, for the 999,998 rest of us, it works out like this: To gain anything worth having, you have to work at it.

Downhill

If you don't work at it, you automatically slide downhill.

Stop working, stop trying, sit down and just coast, and bad things start to happen.

See what happens when you stop going to work for three weeks. You lose your job. The money stops coming in. Sit on your rump and gorge yourself – your weight, blood pressure, cholesterol and physical discomfort all rise, automatically.

Sucks, doesn't it?

Good things take work. Bad things are easy. The easy things are bad because they always, eventually, have their prices, side effects that make them, in the end, very hard. The easy route always takes you downhill.

Questioning the things people tell you, and expecting answers, is hard. Simply believing is easy. Taking your dog for a walk takes effort. Leaving the poor little guy tied up in the yard is easy.

Judging someone on their own merits is hard. There's all that thinking and evaluating. But racism is easy.

In fact, any kind of prejudice is easy. All you have to do is look at 'em. They're the wrong color, they dress funny, they talk with hard-to-understand accents, they smell weird.

Racism is easy. Giving people respect is hard. But which is harder in the long run? Which returns the greater value?

Fast food is easy. Fixing fresh food at home is hard. Where's the better nutrition?

Doing sports is hard. Watching it on TV is easy. But who ends up in better physical condition? And really, who has a better time?

The bad news is: The easy way is, eventually, the hard way.

The really bad news is: There are worse things than "easy."

In the real world, you don't just roll gently down to the bottom of that hill after you take your foot off the gas. And once there, you don't just leisurely decide "Well, heck, I'm bored with this," and then start back up.

Oh, no. No, in the real world, there are things that actually *pull* you down. Some things are so far beyond easy, they're almost irresistible. They're *seductive.*

There are things that *keep* you down. Some things are so far beyond easy, they're almost inescapable. They're *addictive.*

There are things that, after you're down, start *eating* you. Some things are so far beyond easy, they're deliberately destructive. They're *predatory*.

Seduction

"Easy" is fairly seductive all by itself. But active seduction puts skates on easy and rockets you down the hill in double-time.

When an advertiser tells you over and over and over that a Big Mac, fries and a Coke is what you want for lunch, when the rich, salty smell wafts out at you in a mall, when you see TV commercials of happy, healthy people enjoying the good times at Mickey D's, you're being actively seduced.

They've told you ten thousand times that Budweiser will make things fun. That a Toyota 4WD pickup will make life exciting. That driving a Ferrari will get you laid. That diamonds are forever. That only a Barbie-thin blonde girl with a big bubble chest can snag a rich, handsome guy. That only Republicans can keep us safe. That a lottery ticket is your best chance to change your pathetic life.

They seduce you to believe that *their* way is the good way, so you give them your time, your money, your allegiance.

And that downward pull is irresistible ... almost.

Addiction

After you eat all those salty, juicy burgers, drink all that beer, and spend all that time watching sports on TV instead of doing it, once you gain 30 pounds or so, it's very, very hard to get thin and fit again. Count the number of people you know personally who've gotten overweight and then reversed course to get back in really good shape again. Body fat itself is addictive.

And here's the trick with addiction: You slide into it on a long, gradual slope – you gain weight a tiny bit at a time. But the slope back up, to where you're slender and healthy again, is very steep. It's practically a cliff.

You stay down because ... well, because it's just too hard to get back up.

Gained weight is addictive. Once you get there, you stay there, unless you put in a *lot* of effort.

Learning to smoke is easy. It takes only a few days. But stopping is so hard lots of people never manage it. You bet your ass the tobacco companies know this. That's why they spent millions, billions, all those years, seducing us with how Kool and glamorous it was, how Marlboro Manly it was, how every woman could be Virginia Slims interesting and attractive. They addict you ... and unless you make a huge effort to get free, you're theirs forever. Gentle slope in, steep slope out.

Drugs: Gentle slope in, steep slope out.

This is all really our own ability to form habits being turned against us. You can form a habit in a few days or weeks, and after that it maintains itself without apparent effort. But to break a habit can take weeks, sometimes years, of conscious effort. Add in chemical dependence, or a braided complex of social factors – you always smoke with friends, or you get more breaks at work if you're a smoker – and it becomes harder than ever to break the habit.

If there are bigger payoffs – you don't have to hear your nagging wife as long as you're watching football on TV, or you don't have to do your homework as long as you're chatting online – you get stuck even worse.

Predation

Whatever they're offering, they tell you it's easy. It's delicious. It's fast. It's sexy. It's classy. It's what the rich, sophisticated people have. And you can get it ... for a very small price.

You can take the easy route, they say, you can coast, and yet *still* get a good end result. With the Ab-A-Cizer, those pounds and inches will just melt away, in minutes a day! This is the diet plan you'll stick to, because it's *easy*. Learn a language *while you sleep*! Make $50,000 a year, *at home*!

You never have to change a thing about you. All you have to do is buy their pitch and you'll be better. They have it, you need it, and all it takes is for you to give them a little bit of money.

What's really happening? They're seducing you into helping them climb *their* hill.

You smoke the Marlboros, you buy the biggest clear rock (ahem, diamond) you can afford, you drive the Toyota. And somehow, automatically, you become better.

The problem is, you step off your path, stop climbing up your own hill, and instead your efforts are diverted to boosting them up theirs. Sure, you're working like hell, so it feels like something good is happening – but you're really putting most of that effort into helping *them* grow and prosper.

Maybe it's not even a "little bit" of money they're asking. Maybe it's a big bit. Maybe it's a *huge* bit. Nobody ever advertised cheap European sports cars, for instance.

But if you have to work all the harder to get it, you feel, perversely, even more strongly that you're climbing your own hill at top speed. Even when it sets you back $80,000[20], you feel good about it.

This is predatory. They're sucking the life out of you. To get up *their* hill, they convince you – and a lot of other people – to let them climb on your back and push you down yours.

It gets even more shameless. Drive through the really poor parts of town someday and you'll find the level of predators there is *much* higher than it is in all the richer elsewheres. You'll see a *lot* more cigarette and beer and lottery ads. You'll find more sleazy little stores selling bread and milk at twice the price you can get it at the big supermarket. Poor neighborhoods are where you find the psychic advisors, the tattoo parlors, the gambling joints, the quick check-cashing places, the "Make Big Money At Home" posters tacked onto telephone poles.

Stay up and watch TV past midnight some night, the time slot shared by the poor, the jobless, the stressed and the sleepless, and you'll be amazed at the number of state lottery ads, advertisements for great new money-making careers in court reporting, courses in how to make millions in real estate, ads for trade schools, ads for Viagra, weight loss plans and pills, home gym gadgets, on and on.

If you're already on the bottom, you're the juiciest of prey. To a *lot* of people. The bottom is where legions of predators gather. The payoffs are small, but the pickings are easy, because the people down there, a lot of them, are defenseless. You can rape them on the long-term cost of a rent-to-own TV, and when

---

20   *You slide down your hill $80,000 worth while they rise up their hill $80,000 worth. Yes, your fall is slightly offset by the fact that you get some useful transportation, and their rise is offset by the expense of producing the car. But do you get $80,000 of transportation? And do you think it costs them any more to design and build an $80,000 car than the $20,000 car they probably also make? No, and no. And this is not to mention the additional ten grand or so you'll give to some bank for the privilege of pushing them up THEIR hill.*

they can't pay for it, it's automatically *their* fault.

Religion

And so we come to religion. (You knew we were getting there, right?)

Religion is easy. It's so easy, a man with an IQ of 70 can get it. Yes, there's a career track where you can strive for advanced degrees in theology, but to be a convert, to be "saved," you only need to submit. Acknowledge Christ as your personal savior. Be baptized. Show up on Sunday. Eat the wafers, drink the wine. Confess. Get on your knees and pray to Allah. Do a lot of stuff that can be done by a person of extremely limited intellect and literally no physical abilities at all.

You don't even have to actually read the Bible.

All you have to do is believe anything they say, do whatever they tell you to do, and you're in.

In fact, religion goes beyond easy. Religion is *seductive*.

If you believe in it, you get to have all your failings forgiven. You get to live on beyond death. In a glorious paradise. With countless sexy virgins. And, uh, your family. And shucks, maybe even your dog.

But if you *don't* believe, if you question and doubt, they throw you out. They curse you. God sends you warts. Brain cancer. Hurricanes. And when you die, you burn. Screaming. Forever. While demons stab you with pitchforks. And everybody in Heaven laughs.

It goes beyond seduction. Religion is *addictive*.

Because it's bound up with your family, your culture, and even your ability to think independent thoughts, once you get into religion, it's really, really hard to break out.

In church, you don't even dare to speak up with questions. Ever see anybody raise their hand and question a basic belief of your church? You wouldn't do it because you'd be Making A Scene. So you keep those questions to yourself, or even stifle them *from* yourself.

But the privacy of your home isn't any safer. You advance the slightest question at the dinner table about the existence of God one fine November evening, and a few weeks later your grandmother is tugging at your sleeve and crying pitifully over you at the family Thanksgiving gathering, terrified that you're going to hell, while all your aunts, uncles and cousins look on, horrified that you could drive her to the brink of a heart attack or stroke like this.

In some places in the world, with at least one well-known religion – Islam – you can actually get the death penalty for attempting to break free. If there was a recreational drug you could take, a drug that would kill you if you stopped, that's about as addictive as it gets. You've got it for life.

It isn't just Islam, of course. Listen to the words of prominent god-spokesmen like Pat Robertson or the recently deceased Jerry Falwell talking about some outgroup, and you'll often find no small amount of hate. All the faithful are invited to dislike the gays. Liberals. Muslims. Democrats. Evolutionists. Abortionists. Atheists.

Once you're under that true-believer evangelical thumb, sweet baby Jesus help you if you fraternize with any of those outgroups. God Himself help you if you decide to actually *be* gay, or liberal, or a Democrat, or science-minded ... or a teenage girl pregnant by rape. You're stuck with what you've got.

Because, *as you already know*, to try anything different is to be ostracized and disliked.

It goes even beyond addiction. Religion is also *predatory*.

We're seeing it more these days, as religious forces fight for beachheads in schools. They campaign to be on school boards and vie for slots on textbook selection committees. In both classrooms and books, they want *your* kids taught *their* religion, at public expense. They fight in court for the right to erect specifically Christian monuments on the public commons – courthouses and town squares. They want *their* religious monuments in *everybody's* public square. Can you think of anybody else, any other organization, that can ring bells you can hear for miles or play loud religious tunes throughout the day on Sunday?

Ever wonder why preachers end up as community leaders? If they were only there to help, they'd be helpers. But they end up as the makers and guides of moral rules. They end up on televised panels discussing morality. They cozy up to law enforcement and elected officials, pushing for laws and rules to guide the rest of us. They help punish the strays with rhetoric about sins and sinners. They climb their hill on the backs of others.

Ever wonder why, in an area where a lot of ordinary houses and business buildings exist, there will often be a soaring stone cathedral, a literal castle, that belongs to a church?

Ever wonder why churches, despite getting the same or better police and fire protection (and many other public services) as the rest of us, pay no property or school taxes?

And then there's this other thing: Canvas the

neighborhoods filled with poor, ignorant people, and you'll find a generous supply of churches and missions. Sure, they're only there to help. But they never cease to take donations or government handouts, they're never shy about asking for unpaid volunteers, and they don't want you to leave.

It should go without saying that televangelists are bottom feeders. But maybe it doesn't, so: Televangelists are bottom feeders. They deliberately, consciously, prey on people who are intellectually and "spiritually" weakest. They reinforce fear and dependence with a never-ending river of manipulative lies, and they reap wealth, power and a life of pleasure and ease grander than anything their pathetic followers can ever hope for.

They push their followers down the hill, and they rise up to the glory they *really* seek.

Downhill

Religion is downhill. Sometimes it's a little downhill, the downhill of injured reason. But sometimes it's a greased chute, the downhill of active hate and intolerance, of violence and martyrdom. It is downhill for the individual and downhill for the society where it makes its home.

Yes, if you're already at your lowest, there can be comfort in hearing that things will get better in glorious eternity. But that comfort comes at the price of allegiance and submission, the price of accepting and never doubting.

As a faulty mental model for dealing with the real world, it comes with countless other prices, too. Find the places in the world – or in the U.S. – where religion has the strongest grip, and you will invariably find a higher incidence of ignorance and poverty. Find the times in history when the church had the most pervasive influence and you will inevitably find a deadly dark age. Find a voice that most actively fights science education or intellectual freedom and it will inevitably be a religious voice. Find the person who has the most aggressive, unshakable faith, and you may well be addressing someone badly educated, semi-literate, and poor. Over large parts of the world, poverty and religion fit together like hand and glove.

The Rocky Road

Say you take the easy road. Stop brushing and flossing your teeth at, say, the age of 15.

You'll save all that time in your mornings and evenings. Figuring you'd otherwise brush morning and night for about 5 minutes each time, over the course of 10 years, you'd save more than 600 hours of time – 25 days of your life, just by the time you were 25.

By the time you were 65, you'd save 126 days of your life – more than three months of extra lifetime to enjoy in other ways.

Except by the time you were 18, you'd have cavities. Serious ones. You'd have to have several fillings. And you'd probably have to have more fillings every year or so, and then you'd start losing teeth before you were 25.

After that, figure in a couple of weeks of pain for each tooth until you could get to the dentist and have it pulled, and then maybe a week of recovery, and figure you'd get maybe only half of them pulled before you decided to jerk them all and get dentures at the age of 45. That works out to ... what? Maybe only 48 weeks of pain.

Toss in a month or two for gum infections along the way, then add the 15 minutes or so a day of dealing with your dentures – cleaning, taking out and putting in – and that works out over the next 20 years to two months more of your time. That's a total of about 15 months lost to pain and denture cleaning by the time you reached the age of 65.

Bear in mind, this is not counting the cost and time of dental visits, which would be up to ... what, 100 hours over those 50 years? Maybe 20 grand or so?

Of course, we have to figure in the reality that even people who brush lose a few teeth eventually. But even if the cost was fully half what non-brushers spend, time- and money-wise, tooth-brushing turns out to be a good investment.

Truly lazy people, who want to spend as little time and money as possible on their teeth, might do it best by brushing every day.

All of this is to illustrate the fact that, in the long run, most of the time, the "easy" downhill path is the hard one, because there's always a price. Most of the time, the "hard" uphill path is the easy one, because there's a payoff.

In the real world:

People who don't study in school have to work *harder*, throughout their lives, to have decent incomes.

People who don't have jobs have to work harder to get through life. They have to work harder on their health care, harder on affording good transportation and housing. Harder at being happy.

And people who take the "easy" route, who just "let go and let God," have a harder time, throughout their lives, at understanding and appreciating the world around them. At understanding the real basis of morality. At keeping a clear head when it comes to life's difficult decisions. At seeing conditions in the real world as they really are. At planning and building a rewarding, independent life.

Put yourself on someone else's metaphorical hill, and no matter how hard you work at it, you gain little ground for yourself. Progress on your own hill can't help but founder.

Religion has this price: It can make your life a downhill road.

Which forces you into a very uphill struggle indeed.

HANK FOX

Freedom, Reason & Science

15

In the Nation of Pants

Say we all lived in a remote nation that was so backward the Bill of Rights of our constitution so far contained only the Freedom of Pants.

As a patriot, I know I'd be fiercely proud of the traditions of this sacred freedom.

And so would you, I hope. It would be ... disturbing ... to think you were one of those loose-moraled layabouts who ignored his reverential daily duty and wore just any random old thing that popped up in his closet. Khaki trousers one day, a plaid kilt the next, baggy swim trunks the day after.

As if the traditions behind our glorious Freedom of Pants didn't matter. As if it was some casual thing, an unimportant trifle you could just ignore. As if ... as if you didn't really *care*.

Ugh. The more I think about it, the more I'm sure you'd be exactly like that. I can just picture you, flaunting your ignorance of our heaven-sent right, hard-won on the blood of patriots. You might even be one of those misguided turkeys who let your children wear *shorts*.

You gutter-trash bastard.

... Oops, sorry. Drifted off track there. Where was I?

Ah. Okay, so we have the Freedom of Pants. We live daily in the heartfelt belief that we, all of us, have the duty to honor this freedom by choosing carefully what we wear on our bottom half.

As a dyed-in-the-denim Wranglerian, I would wear Wranglers every day. And not just any Wranglers, but soft, comfortable, free-moving Stretch Wranglers. In fact, all my people would wear Stretch Wranglers. Our fiercely independent cultural heritage traces back to the Great Schism of 1985, when we Stretch Wranglerians attended the Wranglerian Synod and *walked out* in the middle of the debate, proudly proclaiming our independence from the restrictive and arbitrary code that denied us our right to dress and walk free.

However, below our differences, we know that we're still Wranglerians in our hearts. If the conservative Plain-Cotton faction hadn't moved in and taken over the senior council, we'd all be devout Wranglerians to this day.

In the end, we're all patriots. As long as they don't try to restrict our own freedom, we can get along with the Levites, the Gappers, even the Jordachians. The Hilfigers are a snooty lot, of course, and have some decidedly odd practices, but they're still loyal pants patriots for all that.

But this modern bunch, this tiny fraction of troublemakers who have lately intruded with their loud and abrasive voices, I don't see how we can tolerate the silly idea of theirs that the Freedom of Pants somehow translates into the Freedom of No Pants.

It doesn't, you know. It just doesn't. This is a pants-wearing nation, and nothing in our constitution says you can wear No Pants.

Our Founders themselves spoke often of their pants, of their fierce love for pants, and only a complete fool could find anything in their words that hinted at some imagined Freedom of No Pants. And these were men who placed their lives on the line in defense of the Freedom of Pants.

There is no way they would have permitted the unpantsed to walk around shamelessly in public.

Likewise, there is no way freedom of religion could mean freedom *from* religion, freedom of *no* religion.

Except it does.

Freedom More Basic

Are we really only talking about Freedom of Pants? Freedom of Pants is a statement of a specific freedom, but what if it means something more general?

The word "freedom," after all, is a signpost to a very broad idea, something amounting to: "Them big people ain't got no right to tell me what to do."

Maybe Freedom of Pants is one of those tip-of-the-iceberg concepts that has an immense mass of *other* meanings floating somewhere below it – something you never see until you pause and look carefully down into the depths for it.

Maybe what we have is a more general freedom that covers not just pants, but shirts. Socks and underwear. Things like wristwatches and sunglasses. Hats – maybe even propeller beanies!

Though we call it Freedom of Pants, maybe it's really Freedom of Clothes – or, broader, Freedom of Dress.

But surely it's not freedom of *no* pants. Not a complete lack of pants. After all, if people walked around with their bits hanging out in public, offending men, women and children, who's to say what might happen?

Well, you could certainly wear no pants in private. When you were showering and so forth. This is not a matter of some silly Freedom of No Pants though. It's a simple right to privacy. If nobody's being offended or injured by it, you can do pretty much what you want *in private*.

Clearly, based on the concept of equal rights for all, there is a limit to how far individual rights go. That limit is where the rights of the next person start.

Your right to wear no pants ends where my retinas begin.

Freedom of Speech

Here in the U.S., much of this same reasoning holds true for Freedom of Speech.

I'm free to answer my phone "Buddy's Bar, where the whiskey's a treasure and the lap dances a pleasure." I'm free to stand near a busy intersection and yell about Jesus to passersby. I'm free to weigh in on the lack of intelligence in the president. I'm free to go to city council meetings and say I don't want my taxes raised again, and the lot of them are liars and crooks besides. I'm free to say I think the huge, cholesterol-laden gut-busters being served at various fast food restaurants are a travesty, and I would never, under any circumstances, eat one. And I'm free to name the places at which I wouldn't eat them.

In fact, as long as it doesn't hurt other specific people, I can say just about anything I want.

Of course there's more. When we talk about "freedom of speech," it makes it sound like it only applies to talking, but we all know it goes beyond that.

Writing a letter to the editor of the local newspaper is freedom of speech, even though it's writing rather than talking.

Putting a bumper sticker on your car that says "Sarah Palin is a Greedy Weasel" or "Thank You Jesus! (The Lawn Looks Lovely – See You Next Friday)," those would both be covered, even though they might be offensive to certain demographics.[21]

Because what use would "freedom of speech" be, if it didn't also apply to writing? In fact, "freedom of speech" is a cramped way of naming a freedom much broader than mere speech. More properly, it's "freedom of expression."

And that covers a *lot*.

A group of deaf people gathered outside city hall, mutely opposing a policy that only spoken comments should be allowed in city council meetings, deserve to be "heard" every bit as much as those who shout. That's freedom of speech – even if some of them are unable to speak. People protesting political repression by wearing tape over their mouths as the president's motorcade passes, that's also freedom of speech, and it, too, deserves to be "heard," even though they're blatantly not speaking.

---

21   *The Latino community, for instance, but also weasel-lovers.*

What use would freedom of speech be if it only applied to those who *could* speak? What use would it be if you *had to* speak to make your point?

Freedom of speech holds the promise that you can't be forced to be silent. But you also can't be forced to talk.

Because freedom of speech is curtailed if you don't also have the freedom to *not* speak. Perfect example: In the U.S., we have the right to *not* vote. Being forced to vote would be an infringement of your personal rights. We see those countries where every adult is forced to vote, under threat of punishment, as authoritarian mockeries of free societies.

If you can be forced to vote, one of the core aspects of a broad freedom of expression, you don't have full freedom.

Clearly, the freedom to *not* do something guaranteed by a freedom of speech or expression is a completely understandable aspect of that freedom. If it said you have the Freedom of Cats in the Constitution, but your local government required every citizen to go to the local animal shelter and adopt two or more cats, that would not be Freedom of Cats. One of the options that would have to be open to you, if you had the Freedom of Cats, would be to have *no* cats. It has to be that way. Otherwise, you're being coerced.

If you have full freedom of "speech," you can choose to *not* speak. You can *not* vote. You can *not* write. You can *not* sing. You can *not* express yourself. And it's perfectly okay.

Coercion & Personal Sovereignty

Let's take a little detour for a moment and think about what sort of fist lies inside the velvet glove of government: Coercion.

What is coercion?

There's direct force: A cop threatens to taser you if you don't do what he says.

There's indirect force: If you don't do as you're told, a government official reaches into your package of rights and takes one or more away. Your physical freedom, say, or your right to gather with other members of your religion, or your ability to access your bank account. But more subtly, maybe they only take away your peace of mind or your pride, the unassuming ease of your daily life, or the sovereign confidence that you have full rights as a citizen.

If the government can use coercion – physical threats, the restriction of your rights, or simply the looming unease of an implied threat – to force you to do something you would not normally do by your own free choice, you are *less free* than those who retain full self-direction.

There might be five billion cat fans out there, but if you are NOT a cat fan, and if the government forces you to get some, that government has stolen some of your freedom.

It's much more than that, however. On the subject of freedoms, the government has to not-coerce you, but it also has to protect you – or allow you to protect yourself – from coercion by others. If someone attempts to use coercive force on you and the government doesn't step in, it has participated by default in limiting your freedom.

Say there's a free public day at an amusement park, and the only entry fee is that you have to eat a scoop of the sponsor's ice cream – thereby keeping out some kids with diabetes. The government would step in instantly and tell them it was discriminatory and illegal to do that.

Imagine that a corporate-backed senator proposed a federal law that said you were *required* to wear a shirt that carried a corporate logo. Imagine that it became illegal to peel the Ford emblem off your truck or to black out the New Balance symbol on your shoes.

We'd all go ballistic. Even if such laws passed, the courts would strike them down. Because we clearly know we're not here to be ordered to serve as billboards for corporations.

You're free to peel the Wrangler patch off your jeans or the John Deere patch off your cap. You're even free to legally change your name practically at will, thereby altering the personal "logo" your parents saddled you with.

Because what use would freedom of speech be if you were forced to allow others to use you to speak for them?

It doesn't matter who makes the initial attempt to deny you your full and equal rights, if the government has influence in that area and fails to protect you, you have essentially been coerced with tacit government approval.

The government can't take away your freedoms.

But it also can't stand by and let others do it.

Freedom of religion

Just as there's a much broader idea behind freedom of speech, one that might be expressed as "freedom of expression," there is likewise a broader idea behind freedom of religion.

Call it what you will – Freedom of Belief, Freedom of Thought, Freedom of Mind – the government can't order you what to think or believe.

But also, the government can't let others order you what to believe.

And it doesn't matter what type or degree of religion you have or what percentage of the population you and your religion make up.

If I'm a Seventh-Day Adventist, neither you nor the government get to impose your Lutheran standards on me. In fact, I'm protected from interference by Catholics, Jehovah's Witnesses, Protestants, Mormons, any and all other religions.

Choosing None

In the Land of Pants, the question still remains: Do I have the right to *no* pants? Do I have freedom *from* pants?

Actually, no.

However, this is *only* because it impinges on those of us (most of us) who are distracted by nudity. I don't want to turn a corner in heavy traffic and get smashed in the eyes with the photons bouncing off your ugly ass.

But what about in the domain of religion?

If I have freedom of religion, I have the freedom to practice *my* religion. I have a right to protection from interference in what I choose to believe.

As long as I pose no threat to the freedom and well-being of others (the way I might, arguably, if I were walking around naked in public), you can't tell me what or when or where I practice my religion. You certainly can't come into my church and start shouting that we're all fornicators and idolators – not without some legal repercussions.

Even if you belong to some majority religion, with a huge number of voters and elected officials, you can't take over the local government and pass laws to make the observance or practice of my religion illegal. Because if you can subject me to your religion against my will, clearly you have stolen my freedom of religion.

Just as you can't force me to attend your church, you can't use public schools to teach your religion – *your* Ten Commandments, *your* morning prayer – to my children and convert them out from under me.

Your right to practice your religion ends where my right to practice my own religion begins.

There is some broad general latitude included here. You can pray in public, and I have little right to protest. But if your praying blocks traffic, consists of piercing shrieks for hours on end, requires the bloody sacrificing of goats on your front lawn every Monday, or generally interferes with the privacy or necessary daily business of your neighbors, they have a right to complain and have you stopped. Not because they want to put a crimp in your day, but to keep *you* from putting a crimp in *theirs*.

But generally, if you with your religion get to apply coercion against me as I attempt to practice my own religion, then I don't have freedom of religion. You have denied it to me. And vice versa. We both have the right to protection from the coercion that each might attempt to apply to the other.

In other words, I have freedom FROM your religion. You have freedom FROM my religion.

Those damned atheists

Finally, what about those people who have no religion and admit it? What about those who have an anti-religion?

If we have freedom of religion, we have freedom of belief. Of thought. Of mind.

We're free to believe in God, Dog, Allah, the Flying Spaghetti Monster, the Universe, or Zeron of the Twelfth Dimension.

Those of us who choose to do it are also – without fear of totalitarian interference, without threat of coercion or diminishment of our rights, and with full government protection – free to believe in no religion, no deity, at all.

Because, after all, if everybody else is protected against the forcible intrusion of outside religion into their lives, unbelievers and even anti-believers get the same protection.

If Baptists have freedom from the intrusion of the Catholic religion, everybody has freedom from the Catholic religion. If Catholics have freedom from the aggressions of the Muslim religion, everybody has freedom from the Muslim religion.

That means that atheists, by the argument of equal rights, have the right to freedom from religion – any and all religion.

If you or anyone can be forced to observe a specific religion, or any religion at all, in order to retain your full rights as a citizen, then freedom of religion is only a pleasant myth masking a coercive reality.

In the real world, in our freedom-loving society, freedom *of* religion absolutely contains the full right – for everyone who wants it – to freedom *from* religion.

Equal rights, equal time

Finally, because rights in the U.S. are individual rights, religious freedom is allotted specifically to individuals rather than to churches or tribes. Which means that the umbrella of a group's religious beliefs cannot be used to injure individuals in that group.

Freedom of religion is *one* of our rights. It can't transcend or transgress against the other individual rights we in the U.S. believe are innate to humans.

You can't legally force women to get some sort of chastity-ensuring surgery in order to adhere to your religious precepts. You can't force 13-year-old girls to accept marriage to 50-year-old men. You can't have human sacrifices, even if the individuals themselves might be willing, because such acts are a transgression against the very idea of the value of human life.

A teenager can decide to leave the Southern Baptist church and become a Moonie, or a Muslim can decide to become a Christian, and it's within their rights. The teenager is not a teenaged Southern Baptist – he's a teenaged *person*. Other Southern Baptists or Muslims, even close friends and family, are legally bound not to interfere in a way that harms that person. Mild social threats of being denied inclusion in the family Christmas gathering or losing your promised airfare to Mecca would probably never make it to court, but threats of physical harm or the loss of a job would definitely be illegal.

Moreover, we're all free to have our own opinions about those other beliefs and the people who hold them.

Catholics are free to believe that Protestants are hell-bound sinners. Southern Baptists are free to believe the Christian Scientists are misguided simpletons. Mormons are legally free to believe that members of other religions are insufficiently guaranteed of an afterlife and to posthumously baptize them. Muslims are free to believe that Judaism is a mass of treacherous lies. Wiccans are free to believe that Scientologists are as nutty as a Texas fruitcake.

We're not so free we can *treat* the members of other religions in any harmful way, but we're perfectly free to *believe* they're bound for burning hell. We're even free to believe, and to say in public, as are great numbers of those belonging to probably every religion in the world, that all other religions are a lie, a plot by Satan, and a tragic waste of human potential.

Which brings us to one more small detail: The issue of fairness.

In all fairness, anytime Muslims get to talk about Jews on federally-licensed airwaves, Jews have an equal right to be there and answer them. Anytime Southern Baptists decide to post their favorite Ten Commandments inside the courthouse, people of other religions, and no religion at all, get to have their faith-related trinkets placed in an equally prominent place inside the same courthouse. (Or else, in the real world, the courthouse remains free of *all* such expressions.)

That same public trust, that same public access, extended to anybody in the sphere of religion, should be – must be – extended to everybody in that same sphere, including unbelievers, agnostics, and even atheists.

Because Freedom of Mind applies to everybody – not just to those on some government-approved list.

16

The Evidence of True Things

I'm going to make up a story. To talk a bit about Science, I'm going to spin you a fictional tale about Justice.

Robert Wayne Kent, a 40-year-old African-American accountant living in Mobile, Alabama, is accused of rape.

He was arrested by cops as he went to work one morning, driving past the park in which a girl was found brutalized and half-conscious during the night. A black man was seen running away from the park, and an eyewitness says it might be him.

The victim, Melissa Stone, is a recent high school graduate with a 4.0 average, a former cheerleader and prom queen with peaches-and-cream complexion. She's also a lifelong Girl Scout and a volunteer at the local senior home. And finally, she's the sweet, innocent daughter of the town's mayor.

Following the attack, Stone moves into a retreat for rape victims. She undergoes intensive supportive counseling. It is announced that she has been placed on a suicide watch.

Pictures of the 19-year-old victim, whose fondest dream is to represent her state in the Miss America contest and then use her position to work to benefit handicapped orphans, are splashed across the pages of the local newspapers. The story gets picked up nationally, and every person in the country soon knows the grim details of her emotional devastation and her shattered hopes.

Bob, meanwhile, is taken to jail, where he is beaten senseless by another prisoner picked up the same morning, Chuck Weiss, the former boyfriend of the beautiful victim, who is himself in jail after an arrest for DWI. Bob goes into solitary for his own protection but emerges for his arraignment unshaven, disheveled and covered in bruises, including a huge puffy black eye noticeable even against his dark skin. The press prints the pictures, so that everyone in the community can see them, alongside pictures of the delicate, lovely blonde victim in all her prom queen glory.

Letters to the local newspaper ask for a speedy trial and an especially nasty sentence. An organized group marches on City Hall with signs appealing to the prosecutor to consider the death sentence, and when asked why she feels so strongly about the case before even hearing the evidence, the leader of the group says "I feel in my soul that this evil man is guilty."

The girl's distraught mother relates the devastation the incident has wreaked on their family, tearfully demanding "The animal who did this must be put away forever!" The family minister stands beside her and quotes the Bible, grimly reminding parishioners of their duty to resist the servants of The Beast.

The mayor himself appears in a televised interview and chokes up during an impassioned speech against the swine who raped and beat his daughter.

The prosecutor goes to work on the high-profile case, excited that the publicity will boost his "tough on crime" image for the upcoming state attorney general race.

He pries into every aspect of Bob's life to get evidence to convict the bastard. It turns out it's harder than it looks because, as his attorney points out over and over throughout the trial, Bob has led a virtually blameless life. Never been in trouble with the law. A local boy, he was first in his class in high school and college. He's a family man and Boy Scout leader. And then there's a statement by Bob's own son that Bob was home with him at the time of the alleged attack, helping him with his homework.

But then: Pay dirt! Internet server records, acquired with a search warrant, reveal that Bob occasionally browses porn sites on the Web, sites that specialize in pictures of blonde cheerleaders and prom queen types. The prosecutor immediately leaks the sordid details to the press, which crows in 2-inch-high letters: "Prom Queen Porno Sinks Sleazebag."

Bob is convicted in the media, convicted in public opinion and finally convicted in court. He goes to prison for 40 years. Except the guys in prison read newspapers too. Smirking guards dump Bob in with the general population, where he is stabbed and set afire by white supremacist gang members during a race riot. He dies two days later, strapped down and without pain medication, in the prison infirmary.

Letters to the editor pronounce it a just ending to the filthy beast who falsely pretended for so many years to be an upstanding member of the community, and a sanctimonious editorial pronounces the case closed. Beautiful Melissa Stone appears in public with a wan, brave smile, every inch the slowly-recovering victim.

Sounds like justice, right? The guy got a fair trial, and if the jury found him guilty, he's guilty. Yeah, it was unfortunate he got killed in prison, but some people are just animals anyway, y'know? It's his fault he landed there. End of story.

And yet ... the story bothers you. There's something wrong with the whole thing. Maybe a lot of somethings.

So let's look at the forces involved in the courtroom:

There was the "He's Innocent" side, consisting of the one witness for the defense, Bob's son, and the defense attorney. And, well, Bob himself.

And then there was the massed "Nail the Bastard" side, consisting of the county prosecutor, the victim herself through her testimony, community members who wrote letters to the paper, the victim's mayor father, the tearful mother, the outspoken family-friend minister, the jailed boyfriend, the jury who decides his guilt, the judge who sentences him, and finally the prison gang who stabs and burns and eventually kills him.

What's missing?

If we're talking Justice-with-a-capital-J, shouldn't there, in our beloved America, be a third interest group, the "What Really Happened?" side?

Suppose this side might uncover these facts:

Bob had nothing at all – zero – to do with the crime. He actually was home at the time, helping his 15-year-old son Brad with his math homework – the same son who liked to sometimes view cheerleader porn on his dad's computer.

After a year of dating, Melissa Stone had revealed to Chuck Weiss that her family name was actually Stein, and that they were Jews who went into hiding and narrowly escaped the Holocaust. Problem was, Chuck was a secret neo-Nazi, and he was so insulted by her polluting his pure Aryan body that it was he who beat and raped her.

There was physical evidence from the crime scene, semen and hair from the rapist. But DNA testing wasn't even ordered by the prosecutor, and the defendant's alcoholic attorney didn't think to demand it.

Finally, several jurors, in post-trial interviews, reveal that they were considerably swayed by public sentiment, the inflammatory racial nature of the crime, and fears of social repercussions if they should go against the mayor's family.

NOW would we call any part of this justice?

Nope. Trial or not, vital facts that should have been brought out were not. And extraneous factors were brought in that should have had no bearing on the case.

Even though the story is made up, it sparks an emotional reaction. You *care* about what happened. You care that it was bad. You care that it should have happened differently, and better. Maybe you even care about the fictional characters, as representations of real people who have had things like this really happen to them.

Most of all, you care about the process revealed, the unfairness of the legal system that blithely allowed the characters and the community to suffer.

Down at the ultimate base, what you really care about in every court case is this: Facts. Evidence. The real story. The Truth. And a fair, unbiased *process* for discovering and revealing that Truth.

You really and truly believe that justice demands that *who* says a thing should not be the deciding factor in how a statement is viewed. Truth doesn't depend on who says it, or its opposite. Age, reputation, fame, skin color – those things just don't come into it. Reliable evidence doesn't come from the voice of authority. A suit and tie, or a robe of office, does not automatically mean trustworthy and good-hearted.

You believe that *how many* say a thing should not be the deciding factor – facts are not a popularity contest.

You believe the emotional appeal of a statement – how loudly, or angrily, or eagerly a thing is said – shouldn't have any bearing on its factual nature.

You believe the trueness of a thing doesn't change based on how much you hate it, how much you like it, or how afraid of it you are.

No matter how many of these other factors come into play, if the guy didn't do the crime, a system of justice based on evidence and facts should set him free.

Nothing else should matter – not his race, not his profession, not his past, not his private habits, not the things people say about him. He might be mean to his dog and verbally abusive to his wife and kids, but if he didn't do *this* crime, the specific one he's been charged with and is being tried for, justice demands he should go free.

Because we know the cost of unjust Justice. Government is so powerful, even its tiniest mistakes can wreck countless innocent lives.

In this fictional case, an innocent man, a family man, a good upstanding professional and pillar of the community, got what was essentially the death penalty. His family was destroyed. His son now faces, alone, the guilt that it was he who looked at the cheerleader porn, but who also kept silent because he was sure his dad could never be convicted.

A confused young girl was swept along in a media and court circus that kept her from telling the truth until it was too late. Now she has to live with both an unpunished rape committed against her *and* with the intense guilt of contributing to the death of an innocent man. For the rest of her life, she will know she allowed the prosecutor and court-appointed psychologists to badger her into practiced testimony that helped convict Bob. If she ever does tell the truth, that it was Chuck who beat and raped her, it will very publicly become *her* fault that Bob is dead.

Finally, a guilty man – who has succeeded in getting away with two beatings and a rape – went free.

Knowing these new facts, any American would be extremely troubled by the result. In the end, *everybody* suffered – including the larger society in which the story happened.

Even the vile prosecutor, rewarded for cursory, biased research aimed only at getting a conviction, suffers the harm of being encouraged to be less thorough, less objective, in future cases. He will convict other innocents and let other guilty ones go free. Worse, if the publicity helps him become state attorney general, the poisonous influence he will bring into the justice system will make things worse for everyone.

The root of Justice

We westerners feel very strongly about justice because we know the lives and well-being of real people are in play. In the most serious cases, the life of the accused, who may or may not have done it, is at stake. The well-being of the victim, who would want the closure of seeing the attacker punished, is at stake.

Further, the well-being of society itself is at stake – the trial is an effort to gain some measure of betterment in society. It would be better if a real rapist were locked up. It would be better if everyone *not* involved was *not* locked up. It would be better if this victim, and future potential victims, could feel that this tragedy was less likely to happen again.

But how best to achieve that?

Historically, there have been myriad ways to approach the problem.

Systems based on privilege recognized rich Haves and poor Have-Nots. The wealthy invariably gained special favor no matter whether or not they'd done the crime, while the poor were prone to punishment. Coming as most of us do from Have-Not beginnings, this seems especially offensive.

Systems based partly on race recognized and rewarded racial "superiors" and punished racial "inferiors." In systems based on relationships, friends and family of those in power got friendly treatment, strangers did not.

Systems based on dictatorial or royal power might bring an automatic death sentence to an ordinary person simply for being accused of a crime. In systems based on religion, being a member of the wrong church, or no church, might be enough to convict you.

But all of those legal systems have their drawbacks, in that some people would be automatically advantaged and some automatically disadvantaged. To most of us, the one *fair* legal system, the one with no innate prejudicial advantage, is the one that focuses on one question – whether or not the accused committed the crime.

Why? Because no other system can achieve fairness of the type we value, real-world fairness both for individual people and for the whole society.

Being accused is not enough. Being the wrong color, or the wrong religion, or on the wrong end of mob opinion, personal bias, or political power, is not enough.

In our own society, the root of justice is facts. Justice is based on the evidence of true things. Which brings us to this very interesting conclusion: If you believe that true justice must entail a laborious, time-consuming, careful and even ruthless search for real evidence, for hard, unbiased fact, there's something else you believe in, possibly without ever making the connection.

Distill justice down to its core by removing all the business about accusations and perpetrators and guilt and innocence, boil it down to that pure search for fact, to the underlying quest for the evidence of true things, and what you get, it seems to me, is science.

Science is a form of justice – justice applied to ideas.

Science vs. Religion

Crime shows you see on TV typically hinge on forensic evidence. There are cops who arrest people accused of crimes, but the people who do the actual investigations are a different breed.

Arriving at the crime scene, police investigators instantly cordon off the area to preserve evidence. They call in psychics to scan the site with their ESP, mediums to investigate the spirit world and receive Messages From Beyond, and religious ministers to comb through their holy books and to ask God for help in determining the identity of the perpetrator. Knowing that it's all a crapshoot anyway, they also invite in newspaper and TV reporters to give their interpretation of what happened, and local political candidates, to see how they spin it. They slap up a quick voting feature on the city Web site – "Do you believe that vicious bastard Robert Wayne Kent assaulted poor, innocent little Melissa Stone?" – to gauge the opinion of the online community. If they have the time, they give the local bishop a call, or maybe even the infallible Pope.

Not.

What they actually do is collect real evidence – pictures that show an overall view of the crime scene, footprints and tire tracks, fingerprints and cigarette butts, and even bits as small as strands of hair and particles of dust.

Tiny dots of blood or saliva, skin scrapings from the victim's fingernails, semen, all will yield DNA that will strongly support a definite conclusion: Did Man A do the rape, or did Man B? Given enough evidence and correct scientific procedures, the investigators will know, to a high degree of certainty, who was at that crime scene.

Mystical woo-woo is not a part of the investigative process. Neither is political bias, popular opinion, or newspaper commentary. Nobody calls the Pope, or takes a vote to see who looks guiltiest.

Crime scene investigation works, when it works, for this exact reason: It relies on scientific methods and attitudes.

Everything technical works for the same reason. If you want to accomplish any real end, other than persuading people, you appeal to the techniques of science.

But what's really wrong with a bit of faith? Shouldn't religion be deeply involved in every aspect of society?

Let's see.

In science, everything is independently verified. If an astronomer in Brazil notices a new star in the sky, the public likely doesn't even hear about it until astronomers in Australia see it too, as well as those in Turkey, South Africa, Japan, Scotland, and every elsewhere that has a telescope.

On the other hand, if a housewife in Minnesota says on Tuesday that she has been given healing powers by Jesus, by the following Tuesday the faithful all over the free world might hear about it. And without any evidence of any kind, other than her word, sick people will start to line up outside her house. If an imam in the middle East says a writer or cartoonist has insulted Allah, the death threats that follow will arrive in apparent disregard of any independently verified facts.

In science, everything is interconnected. Threads of every science are woven into a single immensely strong fabric. The threads of physics support those of astronomy. Threads of biology are tied with those of medicine. The threads of chemistry hold those of geology in place. Threads of paleontology back up those of biology. What is "true" in one science is "true" based on the verifying support of other sciences.

Science is also a team effort. It is a world-spanning collaboration in which every member of the team works together to uncover objective facts.

Religion, on the other hand, is *not* interconnected. Catholicism is a strong scrap of fabric all its own, with almost no connecting strands to Sunni Islam. Hinduism is not supportively interwoven with Scientology. What is "true" in one religion can easily be totally false in another.

Whereas biology would be seriously crippled without biochemistry, and astronomy would be a shadow of itself without optics and physics, the Catholic Church could survive handily without Sunni Islam. Scientology would gleefully take converts from any and all competing religions until it bled them dry, and be all the better for it. Rather than a coordinated worldwide effort with a single shared goal, religion is a competition, a free-for-all in which every team competes with all others.

However much ecumenical services might pretend that all religions are equal, the fact is that unique religions would not even exist if the founders and supporters didn't think there was some critical difference between theirs and those others – that, in fact, the other religions are *wrong* about a number of important points. The differences between Sunni Islam and

Shia Islam, insignificant to outsiders, are great enough that the two sides are sometimes willing to kill each other to make their points.

Further, every religion alive today exists because it has superseded the numerous others that formerly existed – the dead ones which are now "mythology."

In science, everything depends on concrete evidence. Nothing is taken on faith.

In religion, everything depends on holy books and prophets. The blithe pronouncements of leader figures meet up with the simple uncritical belief of followers. Religion operates by hearsay and opinion, and deliberately avoids the careful examination of facts. There are no independent forensic investigators in religion.

A scientific authority is someone who produces useful work in his field, has deep knowledge of the subject, and never claims anything that can't, at some point, be backed up by independent evidence gathered by others. If you claim to be an expert in physics, people will belligerently quiz you to find out. A man appearing on a television talk show claiming to be a scientific authority *would* absolutely be outed as a fraud in a short time if he was not an authority.

A religious authority can be anyone who leads a flock of believers or is backed by a larger religious organization. If you claim to be an expert in religion – or even personally privy to the private thoughts of the Creator of the Universe (!) – you're totally immune from any seriously damaging challenge.

As I said earlier, science is open-source. Anyone can collect data, do experiments, or make connections. Even children in elementary school, while they don't do cutting-edge research, can at least prove basic tenets of science on their own. A few drops of liquid glycerin on crystals of potassium permanganate produces fire. Falling objects accelerate at 32 feet per second squared. Water breaks apart under a properly-applied electric current into gaseous hydrogen and oxygen. Green plants require sunlight to survive.

Religion is closed-source. In the Catholic Church, only the Pope, the supreme leader of the faith, is allowed to make absolute statements about it. A bishop disagreeing with the Pope could face expulsion from the church.

For a student attempting to objectively test some specific aspect of his faith, not only would he have no physical apparatus to perform the test, but he'd likely be chastised even for proposing a serious question. Churches do not allow independent testing.

Science is so exacting that every branch of it is undergirded by mathematical equations. But there are no equations in any holy book you ever saw. Nothing in religion is firm enough to produce mathematics beyond the number of butts in seats this Sunday, or the total take in the collection plates.

Every fact and theory of science is forever open to the challenge of new data, new discoveries, new refinements. Yet the basic body of science is so strong that it takes legendary effort to deny even small parts of it.

The basic tenets of each religion are not open to question. They are set, and change slowly if at all. Yet the basic body of each religion is so weak that the catalog of religions lapsed into "myth" is as long as your arm, and even unassisted teenagers can reason their way out of religious faith.

Science proceeds through dispassionate rational work. As far as I know, no scientist has ever deliberately flown a plane into a building – because none of them would want to. The supremely irrational mindset needed to fly a suicide mission into an occupied building probably can't even exist in a mind devoted to science.

Religion proceeds by passion. Though the picture projected by each religion is peaceful and loving, religious believers are perfectly free to be smug, impulsive, ignorant, self-centered, prejudiced and insular, and much of religion is driven by fear. Even mild religious observances, such as those from my own Southern Baptist upbringing, can be marked by shouting and crying. And it's not hard to find news camera footage – in this year of 2010 – of religious observances elsewhere in the world that show believers whipping their backs to bloody froth, screaming in rage at unbelievers, and even suicide-bombing imagined enemies.

Science proceeds by embracing the new – new ideas, new research, new discoveries, new evidence.

Religion proceeds by embracing the old, sometimes the ancient. New ideas are so reluctantly allowed that it was 99 years after Galileo died under house arrest before the Vatican allowed his complete scientific works to be published, and 350 years before anyone thought to apologize for what happened to him.

How do we know what the rocks on the moon are like? Science, not religion. How do we know what the distant stars are? Science, not faith. How did we find out how to deal with rabies? Science, not prayer. How do we know how the heat and light come about in the sun? Science, not holy books.

How do we know that dinosaurs existed, and how long ago, and what killed them? It was science, not religion. Nobody living ever saw a dinosaur. But the fact of their existence is so well documented – by science – that even anti-evolution religious nuts use them in their "creation science" museums.

Religion is a game of Telephone, where I tell you something and you repeat it to the next person, on and on endlessly, with almost complete certainty that the eventual message will be distorted beyond reckoning.

But science is an enormous game of Clue. Evidence is gathered, postulates are floated, faulty ideas are disproved and workable ones supported, explanatory theories are developed, and in the end we know things we didn't know before.

Finding true things takes a lot more than reading a holy book.

It takes evidence. It takes science.

17

Holes in the Holy

My daddy had this expression he used a lot: "As a general rule ..."

It might be about any little thing. "As a general rule, a cold engine starts better if you pump the gas pedal a time or two before you turn the key."

Or "As a general rule, the grass does better if it's watered in the morning or evening, instead of in the heat of the day."

Or even "As a general rule, White Leghorn hens lay bigger eggs than Plymouth Rocks."

I digested all this in silence for a couple of years, but finally, when I was about 6, I asked, "Daddy, who makes general rules?"

My dad's brow furrowed as he considered how to answer, but my years-older brother, veteran of countless war movies, instantly chimed in with withering superiority: "*Generals.*"

I don't recall my dad's answer, but I do remember I didn't understand it. Long years later, I do. Nobody makes general rules. General rules of the sort my father voiced are things people figure out, observations you make about how things work.

In my young mind, I had assumed they were guidelines somebody important had set in place about the way things had to be. White Leghorns lay bigger eggs because somebody *ordered* them to do so. The lawn did better when watered at certain times because somebody *arranged* that it would be that way.

After all, there were "rules" about putting your elbows on the table or turning your socks right-side-out when you put them in the laundry basket, and those were clearly made by somebody – either my mother or dad.

So all these other rules must be made by somebody too, right?

But they were different types of rules.

One was the type that PREscribed a behavior, the rules that somebody deliberately made up about things like not putting your elbows on the table.

The other was the type that DEscribed a happenstance, such as which hens naturally laid the biggest eggs. Nobody made them up. They were just things people had noticed about the way things worked.

The type of intent that goes into the formulation of the two sorts of rules is about 180 degrees opposite in the two cases.

In making PREscriptive rules, you *talk*. You command, you

demand, you order. You lay PREscriptive rules on yourself, or other people, as a way of enforcing certain behaviors. Elbows off the table. Flush when you're done. Coat on before you go out on a cold day. Don't mow the grass in shorts.

In making DEscriptive rules, though, you *listen*. You watch, you observe, you notice, you analyze. You think up DEscriptive rules from the world around you as a way of understanding the way things work. If you blow in the dog's face, she might nip you. Eat too many apples on an empty stomach and you'll get a bellyache. The mower can sling out a rock and cut your leg. Chickens don't like you taking their eggs.

If you lived on the veldt in Africa, you definitely would have made DEscriptive rules about lions, "general rules" that you'd share with your tribesmen so that as few as possible of you would get devoured, such as "Lions will definitely kill and eat you if they catch you traveling alone and unarmed."

You'd also have PREscriptive rules for each other as a result of what you learned about lions: "Never travel in groups of less than three, and everybody away from the village must carry a sharp spear at all times."

Of course, you might walk out among the lions and present *them* with a list of PREscriptive rules: "Ahem. You lions, listen up! I have this list of demands. (1) You shall not at any time eat me or my fellow tribesmen. (2) After humans make a kill, you shall not approach the site until we've taken all the best cuts of meat. (3) You shall never ... Aieee! Urk!"

Which would result in a yet another PREscriptive rule: Don't lecture the lions.

To sum up:

We make PREscriptive rules *for* each other.

We make (discover, really) DEscriptive rules *about* other things.

Living out there on the veldt, it would be important to know what lions were really like. How they hunted. How they hid. How they cooperated. What they were afraid of, and what they weren't. When they rested and where. How hard they were to drive off a kill, or even how to kill them and whether or not they were good to eat. You'd want to know how lions reacted in every circumstance where they crossed paths with you and your fellow humans.

Young men and women in the tribe would listen avidly as their elders shared the verbal "handbook" of rules about lions, a collection of both DEscriptive and PREscriptive rules. There would be similar sets of rules about crocodiles and hyenas, water buffalo and zebras, plus rules about all the other predators, prey, pests, plants, and even building materials such as grasses, leaves and mud.

"Don't drink from a stream without first checking to make sure there's not a rotting carcass in the water just upstream" would clearly be a PREscriptive rule, a command about how people should act, but it would just as clearly be based on a vital DEscriptive rule: "If you drink water just downstream from a rotting carcass, it will make you really sick," an observation about the way things work.

Though they might be collected together in an actual handbook (when writing eventually came along), the two types of rules would remain very different. The mind-set that goes into one is the complete opposite of the mind-set that goes into the other. One is a way to *command*, the other is a way to *understand*.

This aspect of mental approach is really what's on my mind here. Because the two approaches of PREscriptive and DEscriptive rule-making pretty much delineate the basic differences of approach between religion and science.

And the mistake certain religious people make, in considering religion and science, is to mix up the two.

A minister might say "The lion and the lamb shall lie down together." And that would be a PREscriptive statement supposedly handed down from a supernatural superbeing.

But an observer of nature, a scientist, would more accurately echo the real world DEscriptive sentiments of comedian Woody Allen: "The lion and the lamb shall lie down together, but the lamb won't get much sleep."

The minister's flock might *want* to believe some friendly fantasy story that lions and lambs might someday lie down together. He might PREscriptively command them to believe that it will happen that way.

But in the real world of the African savanna, a biologist would DEscriptively observe this: The lion will be contentedly burping and licking lamb's blood off his chops in short order, every time.

You'd think that religious pronouncements, based as they are on that tiny part of the universe contained in one or another of a hundred different sects' pocket-sized holy books, would be questionable.

And you'd think that the collected "laws" of nature, based as they are on masses of observations taken directly from nature over hundreds of years of careful observation and collected in thousands upon thousands of books, papers, formal studies and exhaustive collections of data, would be unassailable.

But weirdly, in human society, it appears to be just the opposite.

Strangely enough, most of us feel completely comfortable questioning the "general rules" of reality, what we describe as natural laws. Likely because a natural law is whatever it is, but the human *statement* of that natural law, the DEscriptive rule we make up to understand that underlying reality, is "merely" the most recent and closest approximation we've been able to come up with.

The underlying natural laws have remained unchanged, but our understanding, our statements of those natural laws, have changed in significant ways. Over hundreds of years, we've come from initially crude statements to the progressively refined and corrected versions of today.

So we all know scientific DEscriptions can change.

On the other hand, religious commandments (PREscriptive statements) change little or not at all. They're often thought of, even by people who don't belong to any particular church or faith, as unassailable. Long after any of your neighbors even owns an ass, you're still commanded in print not to covet it.

The worldview presented in an ancient holy book, written as it was in a time before science even existed, is DEscriptive today only in the sense that it was the best guess as to the way things worked *at that time*.

Regarding the Christian holy book's worldview, for instance, encompassing mystical superbeings, creation of humans and animals from dust, and stars described as mere pinpoints of light in the sky, the whole story contained in that particular holy book has, a couple of thousand years later, been totally superseded in its DEscriptive power by the much more complex, much more extensive, much more exact understandings of science.

In any realistic modern study of nature, holy books are absolutely obsolete as reliable sources of DEscriptive fact, which means inaccurate, inexact, frequently mistaken, factually false.

That brings up two big problems:

First, in holy books – or at least the one I'm most familiar with – the DEscriptive rules are commingled with the PREscriptive ones, just as they were in my fictional "handbook" for dealing with lions. It can be very hard for some people to tell one type of rule from the other, though, especially if nobody ever told them there was a difference.

Second, and worse, though we may understand that some particular statement in a holy book is no longer properly DEscriptive of the real world, various PREscriptive rules for tribal behavior, most of which probably arose from the DEscriptive understandings of the time, are still presented there. If holy rule books were subject to easy update, they wouldn't be "holy." Thus there are those who still insist, based on biblical or koranic orders, that decent people do not eat pork or shellfish – or worse, that people who DO eat pork or shellfish are INdecent.

The really tragic part, though, is that in order to maintain the PREscriptive rules presented by their holy books, and presumably by their god, fundamentalists are motivated to insist those books are still completely and truthfully DEscriptive of the real world.

They're clearly not.

But perhaps because their holy book is the only acceptable PREscriptive guide they have for living their lives, such people will continue to say that the complete text of their tribal rule book is factually DEscriptive and must be believed and accepted – or at least go forever unquestioned and unchallenged – by everybody.

They're welcome to believe that. But I don't have to.

And neither do you.

18

The Headwaters of Reality

I n the High Sierra mountains of California where I used to live, there are places where crystal-clear water – cleaner and purer than anything you ever get at home – runs on the ground. It falls in the mountains in winter as delicate white flakes, compresses down to rock-hard frozen snowpack that can be 20 or more feet deep in places, and runs all summer, as it gradually melts, in splashing, rippling ice-cold creeks.

You can't find water that pure down in the flatlands. Why? Because you only get pure water at the source.

The reason is simple: The farther water runs down a streambed, the more chance it has to pick up silt, decayed organic matter, parasites or, once you get close to cities, actual pollutants like industrial wastes.

But even up in the mountains, you don't just drink from a creek without hiking a short distance upstream to check things out. Because, again, it's always possible a deer died and fell into the water up there, or that some other large animal crapped in it, which means the water you were thinking about drinking could be bad, despite being crystal clear.

Generally speaking, though, the closer you approach the headwaters of a river, the cleaner and purer the water. And the farther you get downstream, the dirtier and murkier – the more polluted – it usually is.

Reality is like that, too. Given the nature of human society, the closer you get to the headwaters of reality, the more pure, true facts you're able to learn. The farther away you get, the less.

But where are the headwaters of reality? Let's take a look.

Look at a stranger standing at a bus stop. At first glance, he's just some guy with an overcoat and a briefcase. But engage him in conversation and you find he's a defense attorney with two kids and an annoying mother-in-law, fond memories of his days as an aspiring Olympic track and field athlete, a passion for baking, three golden retrievers he takes hiking every weekend, and the lifelong ambition to do stand-up comedy.

The cover of a book is one thing – a simple, artsy come-on to get you to buy it. But inside is an intricate story, a cast of quirky, interconnected characters ready to play out their mysterious lives on the stage of your mind.

I'm sure you get the idea: Generally, if you look only at the superficial surface of a thing, you're missing out on the complexity hidden inside it. If all you've seen is the exterior of a thing, you've really made little or no headway in understanding

– or even noticing – its *real* nature.

The rule probably leads all the way down to – here you should cue a deep voice and echo effects in your head as you read – The! ... Ultimate! ... Nature! ... Of! ... Reality!

Is there such a thing? There has to be, doesn't there? I mean, say you zoom in on a thing, and you keep zooming in, eventually there's a place where you stop being able to zoom in. A place where there isn't any more "in" to zoom to. You've reached the innermost in-ness, and all you can see is ... quarks or whatever. Somewhere down there, as deep in as you can go, is ... something. The ultimate-farthest-in place where there's nowhere to go but out.

Ultimate Reality has to do with the most basic structure of the thing – the particles, the fields, the charges, the spins, the strings, the dimensions, all that stuff somewhere within it, all of the reality, the information, the full, inner nature.

For most of history, human beings were walled off from it, kept from how much of it they could know. Mainly, this was the result of our own sensory limitations, but another part of it was a simple, ignorant mistake we often let ourselves make.

Take a block of granite: A polished cube, three feet on a side, mostly grainy gray but with some interesting swirls of pink and darker gray in it. Set it up on a plinth so it looks like an exhibit in a museum, and then get people to walk around it and tell you what they see.

Now imagine that on one side of it, the swirls are suggestive, to many of these human viewers, of a human face. And not just any face, but (cue the echo effect again) The! ... Face! ... Of! ... JEEEEEzusss!

You might have a reporter there tomorrow, a national-scale human interest story streaming onto the Web the day after, and weeping pilgrims showing up to light candles and pray over it the next.

All over a block of granite.

Take a step back and look at the overall situation – not the block of granite, but how we see it. There's a sort of conceptual stream that flows downward from the original block of granite.

First, there's the original object under consideration, the block itself, on display.

What flows down from it is a sensory *impression* of the original thing, the raw sensory data delivered by our eyes and hands and such, that comes into our brains.

Just downstream is some automatic processing that takes place in our heads, the *perception* that causes us to see a face.

What our senses pick up and the processing that goes on in our heads is automatic: We see the block of granite, and our brains' perceptual nature picks up the face.

But next, there's a *conception*: Some viewers see not just a face, but the face of Jesus. At this spot in the stream, based on individual history and desire, there's some deliberate reading of meaning into the thing. The viewer creates the meaning in his head and adds it to the original picture.

Next might follow even more added meaning, a fanciful *conclusion*: It's a miracle!

That can be closely followed by ripple after ripple of elaboration and embellishment flowing down from the original block:

Jesus sent this miracle to bring hope to the world.

I heard the Face healed a woman dying of cancer.

I read the Pope is considering a declaration that this is a true Holy Visitation, and has ordered a commission to investigate the many miracles attributed to this Jesus of the Rock.

Every new pip of an idea flows down from the ones before it, until the true nature of the original block is so far missing from the stream of discussion that it becomes almost irrelevant. Fanciful stories associate the block with miracles, disembodied voices, angelic presences, mystical interpretations, group imaginings, and on and on, so that the original block of granite recedes in importance to near zero.

See what I mean by downstream? Every step along the way creates additional human meaning, which diverges more and more widely from the original true nature of the block.

Each new wave of viewpoint is based on what has been said before but adds a new twist or interpretation. As the block is what we're talking about, it should be the most important part of the discussion – but many of us will instead use what's been said about it as our taking-off point.

In the case of this granite block, the picture we end up with starts with the block, flows down to human perception, then down to human conception, then down to human fancy and storytelling, each step deliberately adding something to create a conceptual overlay – an elaborate human mind-picture – that may diverge wildly from the real thing.

In this case, we'd come closest to appreciating the true nature of the block only in those first quiet moments of original perception: "Hey look, it's a big stone block!" After the mystics and storytellers get involved, though, forcing a down-flowing river of subjective meanings into it, things get muddier and muddier, until the people who hear about it later might have no knowledge of the block at all, only that some divine miracle occurred.

The Sensory Curtain

One very important thing to realize is that *all of these mind-images of the block proceed from an initial inspection by unaided human senses.*

Until only a few hundred years ago, that was the best we could do. The resolving power of the human eye, or the sensitivity of our other senses, was as close as we could ever get to catching on to the true nature of the block.

In other words, there was a barrier to understanding the deeper nature of the block, a barrier based on the limitations of our senses. Everything upstream of that barrier – call it the Unaided Senses Barrier – was totally unavailable to us. We could *only* deal with such a granite block based on human senses, and all the perception, conception and storytelling that flowed down from it.

It's as if our mountain creek at the beginning of this chapter had a high wall across it, a barrier that marked the place farthest upstream that we were able to venture. We could see everything downstream, but nothing upstream.

Within the past several hundred years, though, the amplifying ability of science began to kick in: We started giving ourselves powerful new senses.

With chemistry, we suddenly had something like a vastly improved sense of taste to examine the makeup of the block.

Magnifying lenses and then microscopes were invented, and we suddenly had an intense new type of vision, to peer into the structure of the block at a level never before seen.

See what happened? In all the time before, we had this one choice: Start at the sensory barrier, and move downstream from it. But suddenly we could start at the sensory barrier and move a little bit *upstream* from it. Rather than drifting farther and farther away from the block, we could now look a bit deeper *into* it. We could gain more information about the true nature of the block than ever before.

For tens of thousands of years, we were stopped at the level of human senses, but suddenly we were able to see past that limitation, deep into information-rich new domains, where we learned things we couldn't have even dreamed about before.

Spectroscopy came along, and X-ray technology, and nuclear chemistry – powerful new visions and tastes. Geology came about, and we started to be able to see the block in its natural context of time and place and distant-past formative processes – still more information that was formerly hidden from us.

We forged inward with physics, imagining and then documenting the nature of the block at the atomic and then sub-atomic level. We thought up new theoretical constructs, conceptual tools based on what we were able to discover and prove, and came to understand even more of the inner, deeper nature of the block.

Finally, today, we're at a very deep level of understanding based on elementary particles and various invisible forces reacting together in strange and interesting ways.

With the new technological and scientific senses of today, we've zoomed inward – and upstream – far beyond the historic limits of our natural senses, until we now know a vast amount more about the true nature of things than people only a hundred years ago *could* know.

Wish vs. Know

Let me restate something said earlier. Pre-scientific understanding had this big problem built into it: By layering on mysticism and religion, we were able to appreciate *less* of the block than our senses could originally detect. Once we left behind the picture gained by our initial sensory perceptions and began to embroider it with fanciful stories, we zoomed downstream from the original block and lost all hope of understanding its true nature. We blinded ourselves with stories.

And we blinded everybody else, too. Every added story colored the impressions of all those who had only the verbal descriptions to know about the block, so that they would have no chance even at a superficial human-senses-only picture of the thing. It's as if every fanciful elaboration was a cow pie thrown into the water, so that everybody downstream had to taste it.

The point of this is that religion and mysticism, rather than illuminating reality, fog it up so much we end up with drastically lessened, crucially crippled sense of what the real world is like.

If I lead you in to see the block but tell you repeatedly in urgent, hushed tones that the block is the omnipotent all-seeing power of God given physical form and that the second you step into its presence, all your darkest secrets will be revealed ... you might just wet your pants, or even pass out. That would make it very unlikely you'd be able to assess the actual physical attributes of the thing.

Reason, and a science based on it, are the only tools that allow us to begin to understand the real world. Only with science and reason were we able to reverse things – to not only negate those old-timey fanciful stories, but to close in on the inner nature of the block, zooming past the Unaided Senses Barrier and racing literally to the heart of the matter, to see the deep, true nature of the thing.

Fanciful non-scientific explanations now diverge so widely from real understanding that they actually poison any effort at real understanding. *Mystical embellishment – religion – gets in the way of understanding true things.*

The anti-science push in the United States over the past few years is an obvious example. Conservative, fundamentalist religion makes itself the deliberate enemy of real knowledge and understanding by going beyond skepticism to hard-core – deliberately malicious – lying.

Even aside from scientific understanding, though, just in terms of human social interactions – the hatred of gays, for instance, or a vociferous opposition to any form of birth control, or the automatic protection of child-molesting priests by their church – religion often gets the wrong answers. Religion might seem comforting to some of us, but in any real-world matter, it seems woefully misleading.

In that dark era before science, that point far away from the ultimate nature of reality, the one based purely on the unaided human senses and uneducated human intelligence, that was the best they had any chance of getting to. Which meant they had to start well downstream from the true nature of things.

There were sharp limits on what even the best-educated of that time could find out. Pluck a couple of absolute geniuses out of that time and drop them down in the game show "Are You Smarter Than a Fifth Grader?" and the kids would take home all the prizes.

People from that time couldn't have guessed that Earth has a molten iron core if their entire civilization had depended on it. They had no idea about continental drift, or how mountains come to be. They didn't know why seasons happened. They didn't know we were related to other living things. Other than that it was a bright light in the sky, they didn't even know what our own sun was.

Any intelligent fifth-grader today probably knows more about the way the real world works than the most brilliant person of that time.

Compared to today, their ignorance was massive. Compared to today, they were blind and deaf – they knew the world in only the most superficial way.

Think how far upstream we are from them, how much farther we've gotten in understanding the basic nature of reality. What we know today is that the real world is connected in a reasonable way. Not a magical way, a *reasonable* way. And those connections are right out in the open.

Today we can actually figure out those connections, learning at the same time even more true facts. One of those true facts is that nothing is deliberately hidden from us; there's nothing we were not "meant" to know. People from hundreds or thousands of years ago may have felt themselves surrounded by secrets, but this was only because, with their limited human senses, they couldn't see deep enough into things.

The immense problem for those today who "believe" in the Bible or the Koran, or countless other holy books, is that those books were written in that dark, ignorant time. All the "holy" books came to us from that long period when we had nothing but our limited human senses. Even the most recent holy books – the Book of Mormon, for instance – take the same mystical tone as their predecessors in order to seem legitimate.

Being generous, we might give holy book authors credit for trying. But being honest, we have to admit they were flat-out wrong about a helluva lot.

Drinking from the source

Say you lived downstream a considerable distance from that sweet, pure water of the mountains, and all you had nearby for water was a murky, muddy river. Would you be willing to have some of that pure water from the mountains piped down to you?

Darned right you would. It would improve your life enormously. Your socks and underwear would come out of the laundry clean, instead of just a different shade of dirty. Your iced tea would now taste like iced tea instead of mud – and the ice cubes would be clear instead of brown. You could turn on the tap and pour yourself a shiny, clear glass of crystal-pure, refreshing water.

If you had to compare the two sources of water, would you rate the dirty river water above the crystal creek water *in any way*?

No, you wouldn't. Once you've tasted refreshing purity, only absolute necessity could force you to go back.

Most of the people who lived in biblical times – all those who didn't have the advantage of already being pampered and privileged royalty, anyway – even they would prefer the clean water, if you gave them the choice.

And yet, there are people today who would choose the muddy – or at least that's what they tell the rest of us.

Why would anyone choose water from so far downstream? Impure water? Unpleasantly flavored water? Gritty water?

Why would anyone choose as their life's guide a book written in the era before science and reason and the deep knowledge we have today? Why choose a book written by unwashed "holy" men who could only see what their eyes told them and had to make up the rest?

Maybe because it's easier? Because the water might be muddy, but it's familiar mud? Because lacking the educated ability to travel to the headwaters of the streams themselves, maybe they resent those who do?

In a number of cases, though, I'll bet the answer is simply that they make good money at it.

Make no mistake – few people actually choose to drink the muddy water. Even evangelists drink from the clean, pure source, using cell phones, doctors and jet planes made possible through the use of upstream-style science. But it's the muddy downstream they talk about, sing about. The muddy water they profess to love. It's the muddy water they continuously pitch to the rest of us.

19

The Doorway to Freedom

I distinctly remember being disturbed, at the age of 7 or so and beginning to be an avid reader, when I came across the words "fiction" and "non-fiction."

There was this made-up thing and then there was this real thing, but the made-up thing had its own name, whereas the real thing had to borrow the fake thing's name and tweak it a bit in order to allow people to talk about it.

The real thing – which was everything, every subject, the power of all the knowledge in the whole world – was named only as a negative of this comparatively tiny category of entertaining-but-fake stuff that was just made up in somebody's head.

Fiction. NON-fiction.

It just didn't seem *right*.

I feel the same way about the words "theist" and "atheist." It's as if the believers – theists – are the only ones deserving of formal recognition, and the rest of us are mere also-rans who possess unusual, less-than-human attributes.

As to actually being an atheist ...

It's weird. You get so many people telling you what atheism is, and you're seldom able to really get across to them that it's not anything they think it is, but something so different that it's not even in the same ballpark.

One of the things some people have a problem with – even plenty of people who refer to themselves as atheists – is that what seems to be an anti-religion (or, as some would accuse, really just another religion) is mostly not about religion at all.

Say you're a Native American, and you strike up a conversation with an extremely nearsighted fellow who's totally tuned into racial differences, and he keeps demanding to know whether you're a black man or a white man. The closest answer you could give him, in the vein of ethnic color, would be "I'm not either one, I'm a red man." With some effort (we are talking about somebody dumb enough to care about race, after all) you might get him to understand. Though you might not be black or white, you would still be on the racial axis.

But what if you were an intelligent space alien that looked something like a silvery-green maple tree? If the same race-wacko guy kept demanding to know "Are you a white man or a black man?" there really would be no answer you could give him that would fit into his mental framework. Not only would you not be anywhere on the black-white spectrum, you couldn't even satisfy him by saying "I'm a green man," because the "man" part wouldn't apply either.

In the same way, many religious people would insist that atheism is – has to be – nothing more than a direct assault on their particular religion, or their specific god.

But for me, the journey of atheism was about religion for only as long as it took me to get religion completely out of my head, and then it turned out to be nothing at all about religion.

Atheism is not on the "spiritual" axis at all. It's a philosophical stance that starts in the religious domain, but it stays there only long enough for its new owner to cut loose the anchor of religion and sail off into whole oceans of totally different types of thought.

Is an auto mechanic an atheist when, wholly caught up in replacing a wheel bearing, he fails to consider God's will? Is a writer an atheist as he creates a fantasy world in his head and translates it to paper, never once thinking about the Baby Jesus or the Virgin Mary? Is a dancer an atheist during the moments she sweats and exerts herself on stage, and nothing approaching religion enters her head?

Personally, I'd say they are. What's more, they don't *need* to believe in a god in those focused moments. (But then again, they don't *ever* need to believe in a god.)

We all know that bringing God into auto mechanics, suggesting that it must have some religion-related stance, even if it does nothing more than ignore the subject (and also, by the way, the subjects of chili cookoffs, performing bears and Harry Potter) is a bizarre reach.

What we don't know is that the basic mindset behind

atheism itself is equally non-religion-related.

I suppose the reason atheism has never really caught hold and established itself as a "church" or even some kind of political force – despite the great numbers of people in the west who are not religious – is that it's not really a "thing" in itself the way a religion is a thing in itself.

Atheism has no leaders, it has no organization (although there are atheist organizations and they have leaders, none of them define atheism in any final way), it has no handbook, it has no truly well-defined existence.

To me, atheism is more a doorway between things than it is a thing in itself. What that doorway stands between is religion on one side and a universe of other ways of thinking on the other side – ways of thinking that have nothing to do with religion because they never even consider religion.

After all, it's not like atheists go through their day saying "God doesn't exist, God doesn't exist." For most, it's more like they never think about a god at all. Like that part of the brain that thinks about gods in goddy people is not even in the brain of an atheist. Things altogether different occupy the minds of atheists – things that you could call non-goddy or anti-goddy only if you are operating from a solidly goddy mind-set, thinking in goddy terms, and trying to describe what atheism looks like from your narrow religious viewpoint.

Talking to a Christian acquaintance some time back, I was trying to illustrate the point. Our society is so immersed in religion, specifically Christianity, that it's difficult to find clear ground to think about the subject.

Sometimes, even to we atheists, it can seem that atheism

is merely some kind of attack, a negative argument that exists specifically and solely to oppose Christianity. If atheism owes its existence to Christianity, so the argument goes, if without Christianity there would be no atheism, then atheism is only a pale reflection of the *real* thing, which is Christianity.

Afloat on the deep and boundless ocean of Christianity, everything gets splashed, drenched, tainted, colored by Christian argument: "Atheism is a type of religion." "Science is a religion." "Atheism is mere rebellion, and atheists actually believe in Jesus, they just won't admit it." "Why do you atheists hate God so much (and by hating Him, actually express deep belief in Him)?"

From that direction, everything is GodGodGod, and any absence of God has to be anti-God.

But somewhere out there in the conceptual universe, far away from our choppy, storm-tossed cultural sea filled with Christianity, there is a calm, quiet place where this argument really should take place, if we want to clarify the true relationship between atheism and Christianity.

This calm place is what I was searching for. I wanted to provide some idea of what it might be like to have a head clear of religion, just for a few minutes, so you could get a simpler, more truthful view of what atheism really is, what it really means.

Imagine that you, a good Christian, are on vacation in Doruno. (It's an island I just made up, exactly like New Guinea except there's nobody living there who will be insulted by me using them as an example.)

By accident, you happen to meet this old man from the

depths of the jungle, a guy who's never been out in the modern world before.

He's suddenly standing there on the edge of the forest, never had a bath in his life, not only dripping with filth but comfortable in it, and reeking like a hog three days dead. He wears a loincloth made out of untanned rat skins, greasy feathers from a variety of birds in his matted hair, and a belt sporting a collection of small dead mammals – his lunch. His huge childlike grin is filled with blackened teeth.

Picture that, through an interpreter, this scrawny, unwashed, half-starved little primitive tells you and your tour group all about his religion – his deep belief in Palulu, the god of his tribe.

Palulu appears to his people as a small hairy beast that flits through the trees, and watches everything men do. Palulu, through his priest, the Dola-mimim-u-Palulu, demands that each adult male tap with his right hand every fifth tree he passes, anytime he's outside the main village. Palulu commands that half of every omo-toluaat (a large fruit which is halfway between a coconut and a cantaloupe, and which I also just made up) be left out for Him. He threatens that women must be shut away from men for 9 days each month, and that if this doesn't happen, every adult male's penis will fall off. But after the 9 days are up, every adult male must have sex with every adult female in the tribe before the next 9 day confinement. When Palulu is unhappy with people, he sends storms, plagues of rats, and toe infections.

For a second, really imagine yourself being there:
You're listening to this colorful little character, taking his

picture, making joking comments to your fellow vacationers, "Palulu, yeah. Uh-huh. Okie-doke. Right. Works for me." Holding your breath against the stench, you pose next to him while your girlfriend videotapes the two of you standing together. You're thinking about the gleeful stories you'll have to tell when you get back home.

Feel around inside yourself for a moment and see what you would really think about Palulu.

Is there any milligram of belief in you?

Do you have the tiniest fleeting hint of a suspicion that Palulu might be real?

Nope.

Nothing. Not a scrap.

Not a jot, not a tittle, not a picogram.

You have not a millionth of a billionth of an ounce of belief in Palulu.

After your vacation, you'd go back home and tell stories about the whole thing, but you'd spend the entire rest of your life worrying not at all about what this laughable little savage's beloved "Pal Lulu" might think.

Isn't that right?

It's not that you assert that Palulu doesn't exist. It's that you don't entertain, even for a remote, grudging second, the notion of Palulu's existence. For you, the question doesn't even arise. As far as this little savage is concerned, you're an atheist. His religion is *nothing* to you.

But then again, that's probably because you already have Jesus in your head, an installation that always comes with the conviction that all other religions are nonsense.

Real atheism, the mature sort that most of us aspire to, looks *out* at foreign religions in the same way, but it takes a critical extra step: It looks *back* into the mind where it resides – something believers do not do – and performs the same dispassionate evaluation of any religion it finds there.

Back to the Blank Slate

A big part of the wrong ideas goddy people get about atheism is that usually the only atheists they ever talk to, if they talk to any at all, are the ones still standing in the doorway, the ones who still care about the subject of religion because they're still working on – and for some of us it really is work – how to get free of it. So godders continue to think "Atheism is about rejecting God."

Again, even a lot of atheists think that's all there is to it.

But it isn't.

The door-opening of atheism can be a very brief event or – as in my case – a long, drawn-out journey taking years. But what you end up with is something very, very different from what you had before.

Bear with me for one more little analogy, about this other culture, a people very different from those of Doruno:

Once again, picture an isolated island (I promise this is the last one), only this time it's one where people have never had religion introduced to them. And imagine that they have never invented it themselves. Finally, imagine that they totally lack anything in their heads that even resembles religion (this will be hard if you're one of those who believe religion is an unavoidable part of the human mind, but try anyway).

First of all, if they once did get exposed to religion, they'd find your particular brand of it, whatever it is, to be immensely silly, so unbelievable that, if you could finally get them to understand that you weren't making some kind of elaborate joke ("Wait, wait – tell me again about the woman made out of ribs! I love that part! I'll bet she was *saucy!*"), they'd be flabbergasted.

But for the sake of this illustration, let's say they never got the chance to think of your religion as silly because they never, ever were discovered by the outside world. Say they lived for thousands of generations on their island and never had any hint of religion about them, ever.

They would have no connection in their minds to religion at all – not even in the rejecting of it.

They'd be like babies in some ways.

A lot of us unbelievers like to say all babies are born atheists. Considering how small children avidly explore every aspect of their environments, touching and looking and tasting everything, you could equally say all babies are born scientists.

But the truth is that children don't get religion into their heads until it's forced on them via the fanciful stories, lies and scary threats that pave the way. Before that happens, they have nothing of religion or its opposite in their heads. They're simply not on any sort of atheism-theism axis.

Ditto for our island people. Not theistic. Not atheistic. Something else entirely.

Innocents.

That island, those people, are what's on the other side of atheism's doorway.

Whether he or she ever knows it or not, it's the destination every atheist is reaching for, a return to the untainted natural state of the human mind – a deliberately chosen *innocence* from religion.

Taking on the Title

Once you do get religion out of your head, once you struggle to force open that door and step through, you never go back because there is no way back. The day you know there's nothing there, every sort of religion turns into an empty shell, an unfortunate fantasy born of ignorance and imagination, inflicted on humans by other humans.

Going back to it would be like a butterfly trying to climb back into its cocoon and become a caterpillar again. Not even a 10-minute-old hatchling could manage it, because it's just not that type of creature anymore.

Which leads me to one more aspect of atheism, the bit that has to do with "nominal" atheists.

I touch on the subject because you will occasionally come across the person who crows "I used to be an atheist! But then I accepted Jesus Christ! As my personal savior! And I've been washed in the Blood of the Lamb! Ever since!"

A nominal atheist is anyone who says or thinks he's an atheist. I'd bet that something like 90 percent of educated young people between the ages of 12 and 20 come to doubt their religion, and I'd bet well over half of those actually come at some point to think of themselves as unbelievers – atheists.

And more power to them. I wish I could speak directly to each and every one of them and congratulate them on getting that far on their own. And then show them the path to permanent freedom.

These youngsters have seen the door. They have put their hands on the knob. They have rattled the knob and listened, trying to discover what they could about the other side.

Some fortunate number of them will eventually step through.

A larger number will pause there and dither about the thing for a while, perhaps for the rest of their lives. If asked, they will say things like "Well, I'm not very religious," or "I'm probably what you'd call an agnostic."

But some will step back, turn away, repudiate the existence of the door entirely, and become Christians, or Muslims, or whatever flavor of devout believer their parents and peers are – simply because it's easier.

Far be it from me to deny them the temporary use of the title by saying "They were never really atheists."

But I can guarantee that damned few of those people ever opened that door. And not one of them ever stepped through it to that grander, freer, truer place on the other side.

Because once you get there, it's no longer a question of religion or anti-religion, black or white. Going through the door is like breaking free of a cocoon – becoming *different*. Being released into a whole new way of thinking, an unchained way of thinking, a way of thinking that creates the greatest freedom to be your own unique individual self.

As for the possibility of going back through the door and living in that small, confining place the rest of your life ...

You can't.

You're just not that type of creature anymore.

Adding an 'S'

Finally, I'd like to point out a common trap that even atheists fall into, when they say "I don't believe in God."

Our culture is so soaked by Christian religious ideas and religious debate that even atheists make the mistake of thinking that what they're doing is disbelieving in God.

But atheism, the default setting of the human mind, is really a lack of belief in gods.

Gods, plural.

On the journey to get all this goddy nonsense out of our youthfully brainwashed minds, certainly it's fine for us as individuals to publicly rail against the largest local religion – Christianity – first.

In my opinion, though, no atheist should ever take up the gauntlet of arguing against God without at least making the very strong point that the Christian god is just one small, specific case of the much larger category of imaginary characters or mythical superheroes.

Atheism is more than unbelief in any one particular god. Atheists don't believe in *any* supernatural superbeings.

Stephen F. Roberts said it well: "I contend we are both atheists, I just believe in one fewer god than you do. When you understand why you dismiss all the other possible gods, you will understand why I dismiss yours."

Farewell to Unreason

20

Uneven Ground

There's this thing I hear all the time: "Atheism makes no logical sense." Or "You can't say 'There is no God' with any logical justification."

I continue to be an atheist, for what I consider an endless number of good and logical reasons, but also for a reason that is the justified response to this "atheism is logically insupportable" statement.

Think about this: Any pinhead can pop off with any statement whatsoever about the details of his religion:

"Allah commands all women to be decently covered from head to foot."

"God said that we should remove the foreskin of every newborn male."

"By the power of God, these crackers and wine are transformed into the flesh and blood of Christ."

"I don't want my daughter to get a blood transfusion because God clearly forbids it. I'd rather she died – at least it will be God's will."

Legions of bystanders will automatically accept every one of such statements as fully justified, fully approved for believability with the reply, "Well, it's their culture, their faith. They have every right to believe it."

As long as people are talking about their religion, no matter what the statement or its effects, they get the automatic, unquestioned benefit of the doubt, and even in most cases the full protection of the law, for whatever nonsensical thing pops out of their mouths.

Even latecomer Mormonism, with ample recent-historical evidence that it was entirely fabricated by a con man and convicted felon, gets this protection and defense. Scientology, which is known to have been wholly made up in my own lifetime by one man – a science fiction writer, no less, and probably mentally ill to boot – and which is such a bundle of silly crap that it should be the butt of jokes on billboards all over the world, gets the benefit of the doubt and the full protection of the law.

Few would dare publicly say "Well, your statement about what God supposedly wants is logically insupportable. It just doesn't make sense. You can't say that with any justification."

No, no. Instead, groups of talking heads with such beliefs are invited into every government council on morality and ethics. We print their mottoes on our money. They get an advertisement injected into our national Pledge of Allegiance. They can make up five-ton monuments containing statements from their own personal religious sect to display at public courthouses, and it takes *years*, and a judgment by the U.S. Supreme Court, to get them removed.

They can perform unnecessary elective surgery on human babies, and people just stand by and say nothing. Most bystanders to the practice never even consider that it might be worth a public discussion of the reasons for and counter-arguments against. In fact, if you bring it up, most of those who accept it will think there's something wrong with *you* for even wasting time on the subject. Why do you hate religious freedom so much?

In the face of all this, if you make one mild statement – "I don't think there is any such thing as a God or gods" – these lazily open-minded bystanders suddenly become instant experts in steely logic. They rush in like cheetahs going after crippled gazelles, and their confident voices ring out like church bells, practically shouting "Atheism doesn't make any rational sense! You can't be an atheist with any logical justification – it's just completely irrational to say any such thing!"

See my point?

The argumentative ground is uneven.

Drastically, unfairly, unjustly uneven.

Even people who normally demonstrate compassion to new ideas, maverick thoughts, unusual cultural practices and beliefs, slam down walls in their heads the instant you try to question religion. They fall back into their logical-sounding argument for the instant rejection of any statement of atheism.

Atheism, which so many see as logically insupportable, gets special – specially negative – treatment.

Again, each and every religious belief and statement, however insanely illogical, however transparently created out of nothing, gets a free pass. Most refuse to think critically about the statements made by religious people. Or if they do, they do it in quiet voices and in private, and they interweave any such skepticisms with generous helpings of "We all have the right to believe as we want" and "Freedom of religion is the basis of our American way of life."

It's a double standard, and one that too many of us can't even see.

Even full atheists walk around keeping their mouths carefully shut because they feel guilty about the logical basis of atheism.

Millions of people who would otherwise be full-blown atheists self-identify as "agnostics" because, even though they're pretty darned sure there are no such things as 3-part gods and holy virgins who amuse themselves by appearing on freeway overpasses, they feel ouchy about making what they consider to be a logically-insupportable statement to that effect. "Well, if I don't search the entire universe and determine for myself that it contains no Parrot-Headed Jimmy Buffet Goddess, I can't *logically* support the assertion that there is no such thing. So I guess I'll have to keep quiet and allow for the reasonable doubt that She Of The Green Feathers might really exist somewhere."

My point is this: in the loosely-argued domain of personal faith – which is where all statements of religion are made – the assertion of atheism is equally justified.

If you're not going to apply the strict standards of logic and proof to the first one, you can't single out the second one for harsh scrutiny. That would be like waving a white job applicant through while forcing the black applicant to undergo a battery of strict tests.

In this loose domain of personal faith, the two are equally supportable – there is a god, there is no god – and you can "believe" either one with perfect justification. Yet our civilization is seriously slanted to favor one, reject the other. So much so that if you attempt to equate the two, or assert the no-god position, you seem to be radically slanted the other way.

Atheism – in the domain of personal faith – is as justified as any other "belief."

But there's this other domain, isn't there? The one where both assertions – god/no-god – have to pass the stricter real-world test?

I need to go off on a slight tangent here, to talk about the couple of different flavors of atheism.

What I'll call "hard atheism" is the definitive statement "There are no such things as gods." This is active disbelief, the certainty that these mystical superbeings don't exist.

"Soft atheism" is the slightly less definitive statement "No specific god or gods have been proven to exist, and it's a mistake to actively believe in them until there's some proof." This is more like "I'd be willing to consider that they might exist, but only if some supporting evidence shows up."

My own feeling is that, after 20,000 years or so, and among the 8 billion or so humans ever to live on Planet Earth, if nobody has yet provided any concrete evidence for the existence of one or more of these gods, then for every practical human purpose the second statement is indistinguishable from the first. If you're the least bit non-belief-prone, there's no use wasting your personal time on the question of God's existence until the sky opens up and an angry 70-foot-tall Zeus[22] steps down with lightning in his fists.

But back to this matter of logic and evidence: There's an interesting little side-issue that few religious people consider when the question of God comes up, something that lives at the heart of proof itself.

Let me explain something about the mechanics of proof. If you believe a thing, say that All Men Are Dogs, you can't prove the truth of that statement by getting a bunch of your sorority sisters together specifically for the purpose of talking about what dogs men are. You can't do it that way because none of you, come to tell your own horror stories of Life Among the Dogs, are able to view the question objectively. Objective conclusions can't happen when everybody weighing in has an axe to grind.

To really determine the truth of the matter, you have to turn the question over to someone objective. Get it? *Someone who does not already believe that all men are dogs.*

The judge of the statement might decide, after hearing your evidence, that all men are dogs. She might decide that all men are not dogs. She might decide that no men are dogs, or that some men are.

But she has to start by *not* believing your assertion that all men are dogs. Only from that position can she objectively

---

22   *Well, of course it's going to be Zeus. What, you thought it would be that Jesus character?*

consider the weight of the evidence ... which you then have to deliver. If you don't trot out the evidence, and a good, solid lot of it, your assertion can't be considered true.

That's the way reasoned argument works. Every question has to be weighed from the viewpoint of someone who has no axe to grind. Someone who doesn't already believe in the conclusion the proponent hopes to advance with her arguments and evidence.

Perhaps without knowing it, you already agree with the point: No matter how devoutly religious you are and how much you might insist that everybody should automatically accept the existence of your god, if you come into court accused of a crime, you want the jury to start by *not* believing the charges made against you. All of us know full well that a juror who already believes the truth of the charges filed against the accused is not a fair juror, and a great deal of effort is made to see that those people don't get into the jury box.

The only way to be sure each claim or assertion gets a fair hearing is to have a judge who starts with a mind clear of belief in any particular conclusion. A skeptical judge. A judge who says "I don't believe you right now, but I'm open to convincing. Prove it."

Whether you're proving that all men are dogs, or that a Subaru Outback is the best car ever made, or that your specific God exists, that's how proof works. *You start with someone who doesn't believe it.*

Or, given the lack of an objective outside judge, you yourself have to start by assuming the assertion under scrutiny isn't automatically true.

You can't logically, rationally prove the existence of your god in a court that consists of nobody but other believers. You can only prove it, really Prove It in some sort of objective, rational terms, in a court not already convinced.

Which means, as I said: If there's evidence, you have to trot it out. You can't just say "Prove that he doesn't exist." You have to prove that he *does*. Otherwise, it's no proof at all, it's just you and your friends doing a triumphant circle-jerk.

In the arena of reason and evidence, every statement has to survive on its own merits. Religion can't get a free pass. Every religious belief has to pass through the court of skepticism, held to the same exacting standards of logic and reason, as any other assertion of truth.

In other words, religion has to be looked at from a viewpoint free of religious belief, and in that viewpoint religion has to prove itself.

Putting it still another way, the default state of a rational mind considering the truth of religion is one of unbelief. You start with the lack of belief, and then the believers have to prove their case.

Which means: Every time you have a conflict of one person who says "I don't see any evidence that a supernatural superbeing exists," and another guy who says "God is real," it's the second guy who has to trot out the evidence. The god-believer is the one who has to do the proving.

Which also means: In the real world of reason and logic, the default viewpoint in any argument about the existence of supernatural superbeings is unbelief. Which is to say, soft atheism.

Which also-also means: Atheism is *always* logically justified. So ...

People who hold atheism to what they think are strict standards of logic are already demonstrating a very high degree of illogic, first when they fail to use that exact same standard in judging – on that same field of argument – each and every claim of religion, and second, when they fail to realize that atheism – unbelief – is the starting point for any proof of the existence of gods.

So the next time someone says anything at all about their god, we should all chime in with "When you can offer objective evidence that your god exists, then we might be willing to talk about it. Until then, *you can't logically make such a statement.*"

It's only fair.

HANK FOX

21

Hello Mr. Death

I remember the day I realized I was going to die.

I mean, intellectually, I'd known it for a long time. Other people died, for instance. Not anybody in my immediate family, but I'd been to funerals. I'd lost pets.

I went to one dual funeral for a high school buddy's aunt and uncle. The husband was fooling around on the wife, she invited him out to talk, a gun got pulled, shots got fired. The gun was taken away from the shooter by the victim, more shots were fired. Bang, bang, bang, double funeral, story for the tabloids, four orphaned kids. Tragedy all around.

But not for me. For me it was more like watching a movie. Reading a study in human behavior. Something distant.

Hey, I was young. Watching the relatives poke at the hands

of the husband, inspecting them clinically for powder burns, remarking on how the deadly scenario went down – she shot him, he had enough strength left to wrest the gun away and return fire – that sort of inoculated me against feeling it too deeply. Besides, the two victims were themselves more interested in this cop show shoot-out than in their kids. How much sympathy can you have for people like that? Eh.

But many years later, shepherding tourists one evening at the ranch where I worked, harnessing my big Belgian draft horses Duke and Dan for a hay ride and idly mulling things over in my back-mind the way I often do in the midst of physical labor, the idea drifted across my thoughts like a distant balloon: You're gonna die. *You.*

And I thought: Oh. Oh, no.

I got through the night – greeted the guests, happy-happied, loaded the wagon and trundled out to the meadow, sang songs, laughed, toasted marshmallows on sticks around the campfire, drank the wine, laughed and sang some more. I unhitched and undressed Duke and Dan, hung up the collars and harness, let the big boys out into their corral, capped the campfire, locked the lodge, walked back to my cabin ... and sat there alone. Scared.

Me? Me? And, and, um, no way out? Me? Die? Really die? Like ... *die*?

I was totally spooked. Not in a "tiger jumping out of the bushes at you" way, but in a "Hey, kid. I hear Fat Tony is gonna have you whacked. Funny, huh kid?" way. Life had hit a pop fly at me, a long, long arc of probability, and here I was out in left field with the sun in my eyes, standing there helpless as it rocketed toward my head.

Me?

Die?

Yes.

I lost sleep three nights in a row. Lying awake, thinking, tense, scared.

Me. Die. Someday. And no way out of it. No hope. Nobody to plead to.

I never really got completely over it. Even today, it scares me to think it. And I understand, in the same way I understood that mom-and-pop shooting, that some people can't bear to deal with it, and have to find some comforting way of denying it.

They cry out to the gods. They latch onto the glory stories of eternal life, each in their own cultural mythosphere, and they convince themselves, and others, that they're true.

Yeah, death sucks, but we'll be in Valhalla afterward and drink mead and sing songs of our glorious battles in the company of fellow Heroes! We'll be in Heaven and be reunited with our families in eternal healthy bodies! We'll become One with the Universal Mind! We'll sit at the right hand of The Master and wear angel wings and lift our voices in praise! We will be welcomed into Paradise by 72 virgins and will have hot kinky sex for all eternity! We'll cross the Rainbow Bridge and see all of our beloved pets again, Ranger and Tito and Red Dog and Tippie!

Yeah, and meanwhile, we'll all win the Lottery, look like Mr. Universe or Miss America, and be sought out by world leaders for our sage advice.

You wish.

Is dealing with death worse for an atheist than it is for a godder? After all, we don't have the Big Magic Juju Guy to appeal to for eternal reward. We can't fool ourselves with happy fantasies.

On the other hand, it certainly looks like religion is really just one of those stages of grieving – a radically-extended, civilization-wide, millennia-long Denial.

The price of the whole mess is that Denial is a bottleneck corked against the possibility of growth and change. Like alcoholics with family enablers who excuse and support their heavy drinking, we have an established caste of enablers, an economic and social force that doesn't just say it's okay, it essentially demands that everybody else be alcoholic. And two thousand years later, here we are, with people who still believe in Noah's Ark – which didn't just not-happen but *could not* have happened.

So what the hell do you do with the realization that you're going to die?

Back to the stages of grieving: Denial, Anger, Bargaining, Depression, and Acceptance.

Denial: This isn't happening to me!

Anger: Why is this happening to me?

Bargaining: I promise I'll be good if it doesn't happen to me.

Depression: I don't care anymore if it happens to me.

Acceptance: I'm ready for whatever comes.

I didn't get the Denial part quite right. Initially, I squirmed away from wanting to experience the full realization of the thing, like a coyote in a leg hold trap. I wanted so, so badly for it not to be true. But I never really denied it. The realization that it was true, which was my first thought on the subject, killed that possibility.

You can't deny real things. Even if you hate them more than anything. Even if you fear them more than anything. If they're real, you accept it and go on from there.

I also don't remember ever really feeling any Anger about it. It just ... was. Being an atheist, I couldn't even rail at a mystical superbeing, whose fault it all might be. And there wasn't anybody else to yell at.

Bargaining? Who are you gonna bargain with, when you're faced with a natural force akin to weather? If the storm comes in, you just deal with it.

Depression? At the time, I was already going through some stuff, so it wasn't like I was entering any new territory. Even so, I don't remember being especially depressed about this specific thing.

As to Acceptance, I accepted it from the moment I first realized it. The realization probably *was* the acceptance.

What I did end up feeling, on that day and many after, and still today, was Fear.

I'm still afraid of the fact that I'll die.

But I will.

I remember the time my pickup truck got repossessed. I watched it roll off down the road on the back of a tow truck, and I knew I'd never see it again.

But there was a moment not long after when I got to the next part: Now what?

You have to take that same step in every bad thing that

happens to you, don't you? You accept it and go on to the next thing. But if you don't accept the reality of death, there is no next thing, there's only the fearful Now in which you are forever stuck.

If you do accept it, not just as inevitable but as real and final, other things can begin to happen in your head.

So, I'm going to die someday. I can do nothing to stop it. Now what?

Ahhhh. Well, son of a gun! Maybe I can't do anything about death, but I *can* do something meanwhile about life. Instead of wasting my sharply limited time dwelling on a supernatural lie, I can do something about a lot of other things, too.

I don't have to sit and wait for death. I don't have to hasten it by giving up, by not taking care of myself. I don't have to dwell on it. Instead, I can *do* things, things that matter to me.

I can write books. I can travel to far places and see amazing stuff. I can give my dog the greatest life any dog ever had. I can walk lightly on the Earth. I can take pleasure in getting others – all of us in this same boat – to smile, or laugh, or think. I can inspire people. I can care about things worth caring about. I can give love. I can build things. I can protect things worth protecting. I can soldier on. I can be brave. I can fight for truth and justice, for goodness and right. I can eat right and work out so I live longer. I can support scientific and medical research, so that everybody lives longer. I can make my life matter, to me and to the people around me. In my own small way, even with all my failings, I can try to be a hero.

I can't do anything about death, but I can do my best to perfect myself, according to my own personal values, while I'm alive.

And I can do it all in the constant consciousness that I, that all of us, only get one brief shot at this, and we'd better make it good.

Works for me.

22

The Black Train

I hate sitcoms.

I mean, I like to laugh just as much as the next guy, but the idea of coming home after work and just sitting down to watch such stuff on TV for several hours, getting nothing at all done the rest of the day, is an ugly one.

I don't mean that I think sitcoms shouldn't exist or that other people shouldn't be allowed to watch them. I mean that, to me, getting into the habit of watching them would be a profound surrender, like getting drunk every night or taking drugs – the equivalent of just giving up on my life. Sinking down into obscurity, letting age and senility slowly take me, letting my gifts rust and rot, turning from Somebody into … Nobody.

I think there are few greater crimes than vegetating instead of exercising your gifts, finding the best within yourself and building it daily into something special – or at least letting it off the leash for a good run at regular intervals.

Part of the reason I think this is because I believe that, many times in life, there are no more chances. Sometimes bad things just happen, and there's no time to make them right. If you're not already prepared – with savings, coping skills, or a network of supportive friends and family – for whatever life-changing event is about to happen, it's just too late to get ready.

Somewhere out there in my future – and in yours – is a Black Train.

Hurtling toward us out of that future, racing along in the distant dark, it comes closer and closer, huge as sorrow, menacing as fear, black as pain and death, and we stand square in its path.

Unless we see it in time and find a way to step off the tracks.

See, the Black Train is not just any old catastrophe. It's the catastrophe that could have been prevented. The disaster that could have been prepared for, could have been stopped, but wasn't.

If a meteorite hits your house tomorrow and leaves a mile-wide crater, that's not a Black Train event, because there was nothing you could have done to stop it. But if you work for a company that's going through a year-long process of downsizing, and you get laid off at the end of that year while another guy just like you keeps his job, and the only difference is that he spent his evenings learning to use the company's new computer program while you used your evenings watching sitcoms, you just got hit by the Black Train.

Getting hit by the Black Train doesn't necessarily kill you. But it does knock you off the comfortable and certain track of your life, kicks you into an uncomfortable new situation that will take you a long time to recover from, if you ever do.

If you spend yourself broke after every paycheck and one day find that your 9-year-old daughter needs an expensive bit of surgery, and the result of her not getting it is a huge amount of misery for both you and your daughter, that's the Black Train in action.

Though the thing might be a painful tragedy for your daughter, it's not a Black Train for her, because there was no way she could have prepared for it. But you, who could have prepared, who could have stepped off the tracks in time if you'd only started early enough – by saving your money, or by buying insurance, or staying on the good side of your rich uncle – you got hit. And it will affect the both of you for years to come.

The Black Train is the tragedy that happens as a result of your own lack of foresight and preparation.

I mention it because I'm actually kinda worried about our future.

Let me tell you something I figured out a couple of years back, something that scares me more than a little bit:

In the grip of strong emotions, humans become less intelligent.

Faced with a crisis or emergency, we get ... stupider. Spurred by fear or anger, we react emotionally rather than rationally.

Reason, after all, seems to be a relatively recent addition to our primate brain. Faced with a dire situation, our brains are more likely to abandon that untrustworthy latecomer Reason and fall back on panic and rage, the strategies that *really* helped us survive, the ones that have worked for us and our ancestors for so long.

We scream and run. Or we scream and fight. Or we just scream.

We're much less apt to *think*.

Our beastly brain takes over and runs us like a steer in a stampede, a mother bear protecting cubs, or an alley cat fighting for territory.

All that fight and flight is good if you're faced with a sabre-toothed cat on the trail or a swift-advancing grass fire. But in a situation that involves a complex danger, one without teeth and claws but deadly nevertheless, coming up with a winning strategy is much more of a challenge when our every impulse tells us to run like headless chickens, or hit somebody.

So here we are in the 21st Century, faced with global warming. If you don't "believe" in global warming, there are plenty of other possible disasters to face: Running out of oil. Antibiotic-resistant supergerms. Dying coral reefs. Fish disappearing from the oceans. Overpopulation. The rise of fundamentalism. Shortages of water. Accelerating extinctions. Pandemics. Global economic disasters. Suicide bombers. Wars and more wars. The erosion of civil liberties.

Any one person who freaks out isn't that much of a problem. After all, a one-cow stampede is just a running cow – bystanders only have to step out of its way.

But when more and more people get a little buggy, the impact starts to be felt among the rest of us. They run, and they trample others along the way. They fight, and they trample others along the way. They vote for weird, un-American things, and the rest of us get trampled along the way. The chances of remaining an unaffected bystander sink lower and lower.

I actually think we humans have been pretty loopy for most of our history. Like kids who never had parents, we grew into intelligence without any sort of guidance. You'd have to expect plenty of dire mistakes in such a situation, but the craziness definitely peaks at certain points in our history.

Communism, in my opinion, was insane. It produced massive human misery, for absolutely no gain. It could never have worked on any large scale, because our kind of animal just isn't capable of thriving under such a system. It sought to erase individuality and independent thinking and decision-making, and that's not something we're able to do without very destructive side effects.

The Inquisition: murderously insane. The rise of the Nazis in Germany: batshit nitwit killer crazy. Evolution deniers in the U.S.: short-sighted, anti-intellectual, anti-science, anti-American dumb-assery.

The big problem is that even today, certain of our "leaders" think the best way to deal with large numbers of us is to lash us into states of powerful emotion. Political snakes, radio hacks and writers of manipulative books provoke us to fear or anger, so that we'll more easily go marching off to war, accept curtailments of our basic rights, vote for the "right" candidates, or even rise up and stop attempts to make our lives better.

Religious leaders whip us into a frenzy of fear, or sorrow, or weepy adoration, so that we'll give them more money or allow ourselves to be rigidly controlled.

How do you know you're dealing with such manipulators? When you watch them, you have to watch yourself. Notice what you're feeling and ask "Do I get excited or angry every time I hear this guy speak? Does it seem he *wants* me to be excited or angry? Is he *working* at it?" Because if he is, it's likely there's something he doesn't want you to notice, something he doesn't want you to think about. He wants you, and everybody else, to be less intelligent. Less thoughtful. Less analytical.

This kind of "leader" wants passionate killer apes more than he wants intelligent humans. Passionate apes can easily be turned into puppets because they act in certain predictable and controllable ways. Get people angry enough and point them at a hated enemy – it's just like firing a gun. Even if there's somebody on the scene still smart enough to ask questions about his real intent, there aren't enough others left to listen.

It's tough to notice the manipulation when it's happening. You're angry or scared, after all, and there are other things more important to you in that moment.

And most of us, I get the feeling, have no idea that this sort of thing happens. We're in the middle of the herd, caught up in the panicky noise and dust, and we stampede here and there at their will, blind to any larger picture. We never see those people on the sidelines, cracking the whips.

Even reading this, I'd bet most of us still won't believe such a thing can happen.

Because, for instance, we *want* to believe the president (and by the way, I wrote this when George W. Bush was in office) is a sincere American. We *want* to believe he and his advisors are honest, and caring, and see us as human beings and fellow Americans. We *want* to believe Pat Robertson is a man of God, a genuinely good person, instead of a manipulative multimillionaire with a vicious lack of conscience. We *want* to believe that global warming is a myth, and that Planet Earth will heal itself.

I worry about it. Not about global warming exactly, but about the whole picture of "humans faced with the Black Train."

I think if we're bright and careful, and start early enough, we can solve just about any problem.

But in the U.S. right now, there is that powerful anti-intellectual, anti-education, anti-expertise, anti-Reason undercurrent. Bright people, well-educated people, are actively sneered at. Ridiculed. Hated. On national television and radio, by the hosts of established programs with very large audiences.

I worry when I see it happening in politics, but I worry *especially* when I see it happening as the sharp tip of a religious movement. Fundamentalists and neo-conservatives in the U.S. are the same people.

We've forgotten the lessons of history except as bundles of facts. We've been so rich and well-fed and safe for so long that we don't think a lot of those things matter. "People aren't like that today. We've evolved beyond the witch burnings and inquisitions and wars." And yet we haven't. There are places on earth where they still happen. Light the right spark and they can flare up here.

Whatever the future does bring, there's a guarantee there will be some disaster facing each and every one of us, and probably all of us collectively, within our lifetimes.

Some of those things will be our individual Black Trains.

We'll see our car go off down the road behind the repo man's tow truck because we didn't pay our bills. We'll have heart attacks because we couldn't muster the will or awareness to eat right and exercise. We'll lose loved ones to divorce because we never thought to tell them how much we loved them, assuming instead that they could somehow pick it up from our long, cool silences. We'll crash and burn in our careers because we lost the sharp edge we once had and let our skills decay.

Some of them will be Black Trains for the lot of us. Within your lifetime, there might well be a large-scale pandemic, something that will kill thousands, millions, possibly even billions. Within your lifetime, a number of species will disappear from the wild. There will be foods you like, maybe a type of fish, that you just won't be able to get anymore. Rights that you thought were rock-solid, god-given, may vanish from your life.

I worry that, faced with some sort of natural or social or epidemiological disaster, we'll find out we could have headed it off if we started 10 years ago, or 50 years ago. We'll find that, without knowing it, we set a Black Train on the tracks and gave it just enough throttle to carry it on a long, slow curve so that we're just now starting to see its terrible headlight out there in the darkness.

We set it in motion back then, with our appetites, our carelessness, our greed, and we rested. We were so safe and rich and free, the only time we got angry or fearful was when somebody tried to point out the danger, and we either shouted or laughed at them in response, and then sat back in our easy chairs resting square on the tracks, and watched our sitcoms.

We started thinking that good things happen automatically, that rust was vanquished for always, and that we were safe and free forevermore. We read our books, and we nodded our heads at the ideas in them, and we patted ourselves on the back about how great and wise we were, and we did nothing.

We bought the lie that the motive force of our lives is to be found in government, or television, or corporations, or Jesus, all supplied to us by wiser heads, those richer, smarter and more powerful than us, in some distant and better place.

We stand stupidly on the tracks, ignoring foresight, ignoring preparation, ignoring education, ignoring proactive planning and independent responsibility, and out of the darkness, across noisy miles and years, the Black Train comes rushing.

The automatic reaction of a lot of us will be ... not reason, not calm careful consideration, but panic. Raw, screaming, beastly, thoughtless fear. All the worst possible reactions to a complex, subtle danger.

Friends on the journey

If you suspect there's a Black Train out there somewhere, who do you want on your team? Do you want excitable dullards who will either stampede in panic or else calmly wait for Jesus-magic to come and fix everything? Or do you want rational people who, after a lifetime of reason and thoughtfulness and science, are more prone to approach emergencies with intelligence, care and calm?

In the midst of a large-scale disaster, a pandemic or a looming hurricane, do you want people who are prone to sit down and pray, or do you want people who are active and thoughtful, people who automatically take some rational action as their first step in dealing with disaster?

Of course we're only human, and there's no guarantee how any individual will react in any specific emergency. We each of us have our own measure of flaws, and some situations are more personal than others.

But in any situation involving our larger society, the question is really what will be the statistical average of reactions among the entire population. If those reactions are mostly calm and measured – and proactive – you get one end result. It they're mostly excitable, superstitious and panicky, you get a totally different one.

It's not so much a question of yes or no, but one of degree. You want on your team the largest quantity of reasonable people that you can get – those who are most likely to think of and use the Heimlich maneuver when faced with a choking emergency, rather than the ones who fall into helpless screaming.

What this means is that in any emergency, those handmaidens of unreason – the hate-stirrers in the media, the cheerleaders of fear in the government, and yes, all those fundamentalist religious pitchmen – are not the best teammates. They might even be – hell, they almost definitely are – your enemy.

So pick better teammates. Become a better teammate yourself. Promise yourself you'll be a stronger, wiser, more caring, more *prepared* person, for yourself and the people around you. And deal with what comes as sanely as you can.

Standing on the tracks

If you read this and think, oh wow, isn't that profound, and then do nothing, you've missed the main point of everything

I'm saying here: The Black Train is coming. Now. Somewhere out there, it *is*.

There's always a Black Train out there, and maybe you can never tell what it is that you should have done until the moment comes and you think, "Oh, crap, if I had only ..."

But we can't just sit back and resign ourselves to the inebriating pleasures of life in order to keep from knowing that we're standing on the tracks. We can't just rest. We can't give ourselves over to the comfortable fantasies of our religions, or our political parties, or our entertainments.

Instead, we can do things to slow or stop it.

We can buy insurance. We can wear seat belts when we drive. We can save money. We can go to school board meetings. We can eat better. We can get fit. We can involve ourselves in our kids' lives. We can look at what politicians *do* rather than just what they say during campaigns. We can watch the TV news, but then research online to find out if they've told us only half-truths. We can turn off the hate-filled voices on the radio and TV and spend the time instead thinking of positive things to do.

And we can stand up for reason and justice and true things, every day. We can fight against the people who want to stampede us into fight or flight. If we have to fight, better to fight cool and early and long and smart instead of short and hot and loud and late.

We can make the future of our world *our* future, a future of hope and health and freedom, of science and reason, instead of the small, stupid, greedy, violent, *ignorant* future that seems to be trundling along the tracks. We can, each of us, do *something*.

253

The trick is, we have to figure out what we as individuals can do, and then just start doing it.

23

The Village

There's this little place where we humans grew up. It's not any specific geographical spot. It's more a conceptual place, a place in the mind. Call it the Village.

If it was a real place, I picture it about 20,000 years or so ago, resting in a pocket valley that opened onto a huge grassy plain. But it could just as well have been sited at the edge of an untracked desert, or right on the verge of an endless forest.

It's the place we lived as we were becoming our human selves.

Early on, the Village was surrounded by darkness. Out there in the dark dwelled monsters and terrifying unknowns. But it was well-lit in the Village, and safe, and everybody knew it.

We lived in it for countless generations, thousands and thousands of years. Since before we had history, really, it was all we knew.

Everything we needed was there, and nobody would even think about leaving it. But it was so dangerous, out beyond the edge of the Village, that we couldn't leave it to chance that one of us might accidentally wander away and get lost. We put up ropes, and rules, and walls. And we came to believe, and tell each other, that if you left the Village, you would die.

We took the belief pretty seriously. It wasn't *safe* for anyone to go off on their own. It became a terrible crime to talk about, to even think about, leaving the Village.

Because talking about leaving was not only bad for the person who did it, it was bad for everybody else. Such careless thoughts would encourage young people, and the less intelligent, to wander off and die horribly in the trackless wasteland that lay outside the Village. What if a whole group of our neighbors wandered off and died?

Eventually we made it the number one rule: Nobody leaves.

We were so serious about it, in fact, that if someone *did* try to leave, if they even talked about leaving, if they even imagined leaving, we tortured and killed them. In public.

People had to *know*, you see, that every aspect of the idea was forbidden.

Over time, of course, the standards grew lax. Oh, we'd bear down from time to time in our long history and burn or hang or drown a few suspected deserters.

But really, it wasn't necessary most of the time. If a father taught his son the dire importance of staying in the Village, if he made it unthinkable that the son might consider leaving, and then if that young man grew up and taught his son, and he taught his son, and so on, and it went on for 50 generations, or a hundred, eventually the very words that would allow you to talk about the idea of leaving would fall out of the language.

Except even without the words to describe something, it is still possible to think about it. To desire it. To yearn for something new and different. And young people, well, we all know what they're like.

So some people, one at a time, left. Oh, they didn't go far. And some of them we killed or imprisoned when they got back, just as a sort of object lesson to the rest of us. Others we threatened to kill if they ever tried it again.

But the ones who left, they found out things about the world out there.

For one thing, it wasn't all dark. For another, out there it was *different* from the Village.

Some of them brought back stuff. Amazing, wonderful stuff. Weird stuff. Stuff like none of us had ever seen. Foreign delights such as bananas, coffee, potatoes, rice, popcorn.

And some of the stuff they brought back – chocolate! – was not only different from what we had in the Village, it was better!

Well, that threw us for a loop. Our Village elders were pretty much dismayed by that, I can tell you. Better stuff? Out there? No way.

They preached against it. They threatened us. They burned a few people, threw others into the Village dungeon. And they asked the rest of us, "Why?" Why would a person want to leave? Even for an hour? How could you even imagine that there's anything out there that's better than the Village?

But troublemakers would keep leaving. Some people, if you tell them how bad things are out there, they'll go just to spite you. And others just have an unhealthy amount of curiosity.

Finally it got to where the pioneers and explorers got so much good press that people started to frown on the burning and imprisoning. People started listening to those adventurous few when they came back. Some of these vagabonds even started teaching, to small select groups of students, what they had learned out there.

For starters, some of those first few explorers said, it wasn't really that dark out there. In fact, they sometimes whispered – rather nervously, because you just didn't criticize humanity's hometown – it was brighter in some ways than the Village.

More and more kept leaving, going out and exploring that wider world, seeing the sights, expanding their horizons, and bringing stuff back.

These explorers and pioneers marched out and found new lands, new creative life. They found things that were shocking – in a good way. They found vistas that were vast and pleasurable, places that were delightful to the senses and the mind.

Something strange started happening to those who went out. They looked back and saw the Village from the perspective of Outside.

Sure it was comforting, in a certain way. It was home. But it was ... small. It had always seemed to contain everything a person might need for survival and life, but it was also, in a certain light, ugly. It was inbred. Cramped. Restricted. Overcast.

The evidence for such conclusions stacked up as more and

more made the trip to those far lands. It was accepted, in some ways, even by those back in the Village. After all, they ate the chocolate. They drank the coffee.

But the diehard leaders of the Village, that little torch-lit town, refused to venture out and see any of the new stuff in the lands of its origins. They held to their convictions. They refused to go out and see the light. And not only did they not want it, they wanted everybody else to not want it, too.

They continued to say, "The only good thing is our Village. Nothing else can be any good. If you go out there beyond the boundaries of the Village, you will *die*. These pioneers and explorers are *evil*." But all the time they said this, they were eating the chocolate and drinking the coffee.

Eventually, to those large numbers who ventured out and stayed out, it became evident that the Village leaders were mistaken ... possibly even flat-out lying.

The pioneers and explorers weren't evil. Considering all the bright and beautiful lands they discovered out there, and all the great new things they brought back, they were actually pretty *good* people.

More than that, considering the opposition they faced from hard-core Villagers and elders, considering that a lot of the early ones faced not just whatever dangers might lurk out there but torture and death when they tried to return with all this good new stuff, they were courageous. They were intrepid. They were valiant.

These pioneers and explorers were the admirable *best* humanity had to offer.

There was a time when we all lived in that little Village, and there was no way to know there was anything else, no way to know that our little Village wasn't the whole world. But thanks to those pioneers, eventually we *did* know.

What we know today is that the people who still live in the Village live lives that are more restricted and miserable than those of us who live outside.

There are people out here enjoying the metaphorical equivalent of relaxing on idyllic tropical beaches, feasting on new foods and interesting new music, savoring brilliant sunsets on shores that are distant and alien to inbred Village sensibilities.

Meanwhile, back in the Village, the residents drink the tainted, overused water of the polluted Village well, listen to their monotonous Village music, hug their ragged animal skins around them and crouch defensively under the dull, overcast sky, sullenly claiming that the Village is everything and that nobody needs anything more.

"These so-called explorers, they're really just Villagers who have turned to the darkness and who are lying about all these new lands. Oh, sure, we have the chocolate. But it's Village chocolate. Really, nothing outside the Village exists. It's all illusion and lies, meant to lure Village children out to their deaths and to destroy all our good Village values."

Back to the real

Enough with the metaphor. Surely by now you get that the Village is religion and superstition and that the explorers and pioneers are thinkers and scientists and inventors and artists who operate outside the religious paradigm.

The bananas and chocolate are not bananas and chocolate

but things like discovering germs, curing polio and smallpox. They're the useful discoveries and inventions like lasers and telescopes, genetics and microbiology, computers and jet planes, and even mundane stuff like bicycles and sewer systems.

At most early points in our history and prehistory, religion and superstition were all we had. Looking back, you might pity the benighted residents of all those earlier times, but you also have to respect them. They were probably doing the best they could. We lived in the Village because we simply didn't know anything else.

But there came a time when it became possible to pioneer new thoughts and ideas, to make new discoveries ... and to bring them back for the benefit of all.

The problem was, a cancer had grown in the Village. The cancer of Church – superstitious ignorance wedded to jealous power.

How many courageous and innocently curious men and women of all those earlier times were killed by the sullen powers of the church? How many were ordered tortured and imprisoned and silenced, merely for using their minds to discover and their mouths to speak?

Like a 12-year-old boy rushing into the farmhouse excited by the discovery of a new fishing hole chock-full of fat trout, only to be stunned to find himself beaten and sent to his room when he told the story, how many came home gleefully with their news, only to face punishment rather than acclaim?

Hundreds. Thousands. Through the ages, uncountable numbers. Every new discovery and skill was either used by the church or ruthlessly murdered, along with its discoverer.

Yet, eventually, we in the west had our Renaissance, our Enlightenment, when we saw the Village for what it was – a womb, an egg, the place where you come *from*. The place you have to leave in order to grow up.

We had a moment in our collective history when we understood that going out there and discovering new things was not just okay, but good. It was even necessary. We came to understand not only that it was wrong to torture people for venturing outside the Village but that the reverse was true: Nothing good could come of forcing people to stay.

It was in that Enlightenment that modern Reason caught fire, and the seeds planted for real, formally-codified Science.

One of the many reasons science caught on is that science has an actual mechanism for correcting its mistakes, whereas the Village ... well, the Village wouldn't *be* the Village if there was any easy way of making changes.

You can leave the Village for all those bright horizon-lands, but you can't make it not be the Village.

It's with us even today. Welded into our society by our own ongoing ignorance, it has a sort of perpetual life, an unhealthy vigor that keeps it cropping up in person after person, generation after generation.

Unfortunately, it also has its perpetual cheerleaders, agents who actually make money from selling it. Televangelists, for instance, have long used the fruits of science, the sacrifice and courage of all those pioneers and explorers, to lure innocent victims back into the darkness of the Village.

On the airwaves 24 hours a day, they beckon continuously. They threaten and frighten, they tell lurid stories of the death that awaits all those who don't move back to the Village, they finger those evil ones – the dreaded evolutionists and atheists and liberals – who want to keep us from the safety and joy of the Village. "The Village is the only safe place to live, and everywhere else is deadly dangerous. Only by living in the Village, by Village rules, can we have Life."

They rant on, drawing millions with their word-tricks, even in the face of frequent real-world evidence to the contrary: Does it look dark and small and squalid in the Village? That's only a trick of your mistaken perspective. The *real* darkness is in all the outside world; the Village is bright and clean and happy, and everybody lives forever. Do the people still living in the Village look like slaves, smiling and singing fearfully so their masters will let them live? On the contrary, only Villagers enjoy true freedom, and all those outside the Village live in confused agony, the servitude of not knowing the true joy of Village limits.

And because life always takes work and sometimes brings pain and fear, we turn a listening ear to anyone promising rest from the pain, or joy in place of fear. By the millions, the weakest and youngest and least thoughtful – the most vulnerable among us – look toward the Village.

But few can really live there anymore. Most of us in the West live almost completely outside the Village. Those who attempt a Village existence are forced into an uncomfortable half-life between ancient fantasy and current-day real world.

The fact is, there is nothing in the Village necessary to life today.

The cheerleaders say compassion is a Village value, and

maybe they're right. But they're lying when they say it's exclusive to the Village.

They say people who live outside the Village are angry and unhappy. Some of them say outright that if you live outside the Village, you fall into evil and despair, and are literally unable to stop yourself from committing rape and murder.

And yet most of us don't.

Because we humans are *naturally* compassionate. Freed of the lash of hunger and want, we're even prone to generosity. Those of us outside the Village manage to handle the myriad difficulties of life with courage and perseverance, and even make new discoveries on a regular basis – something which does not, and never did, happen back in the Village.

The Village looks desirable only because none of us is *forced* to live in it (at least in Western civilization). Freed of coercion, it holds the lure of engaging simplicity.

Yet even watered down, it still carries a terrible price: It continues to take literally billions of thinking minds out of the ranks of the clearheaded, making every real-world problem that much harder to solve.

Those who look around and say "Oh, there's so much wrong in the world; we need to get back to the Village" paint themselves as solvers of new problems, but what they really are is enemies of new solutions. They work to prevent us from coming up with fresh ideas about what's wrong and how to deal with it. They have one quick and easy answer – go back to the Village – but it's the answer that can take no account of the actual details of the problem.

Though most of us don't live in the Village, and wouldn't,

we're still tethered to it as a society. We're so possessed by Village values, Village mandates, that even today we have all too few who are really 100 percent free. Village thinking colors every part of society.

But if you go by Village rules, you get Village results.

If you accept only Village reproductive guidelines, for instance, you may be "blessed" with nine children, when you really wanted – and had the ability to take care of – only two. If you see your politics through a Village filter, you might well pick the less-qualified, dumber candidate who appears to share your values, rather than the more-qualified, brighter guy who disagrees with you on one or two things. If you accept only Village values regarding sexual orientation, the little girl who was the darling of your life at the age of 12, the person you thought would be your own special joy forever, may be your mortal enemy at the age of 19 – and it might be *you* who throws *her* out.

Luckily for those of us alive today, very few are now required to live in the Village. Most of us live our whole lives outside it. Even those who imagine they're still living in it, even they spend only very short amounts of time in it. Mostly, they go to church on Sunday, they stand at the Village gate gazing fondly in for an hour or so, and then they retreat back to the grander, larger outside world.

I have warm boyhood memories of weekends spent visiting Aunt Kate and Uncle Grover in Purvis, Mississippi, sleeping in a huge bed with deep goose-down comforters and hand-stitched quilts above me, listening to the rain patter soothingly on their tin roof, and waking up to a big breakfast of eggs, thick-sliced bacon and Aunt Kate's huge homemade buttermilk biscuits, all out of a big cast-iron wood-burning stove. I can see the appeal of a simpler, seemingly safer land in which to take up residence.

But Aunt Kate and Uncle Grover lived in a farmhouse with practically zero insulation, they got their water from a well outside – they didn't even have a hand pump on it – and every trip to the bathroom, even in winter, was across the back yard for a considerable distance, where you sat on a cold wooden seat with a hole in it and tried not to think about torpid spiders attracted to your warm bottom from the darkness underneath.

We look back fondly on the Village, we yearn for it, and I understand that. But most of us rightly *choose* to live Out Here.

The Village is not a good place to live. It never was, except in the sense that it was all we had. When we became able to move on to better places, we moved on, and gladly, to better places – places where most of our kids live past childhood, where we get to go to the bathroom indoors, where we can reach out electronically to a community of friends scattered around the entire world, every day of the week.

People given the free choice of the Village or the outside world will almost always choose the outside.

It's no contest. On one side, the Village – millions of children dying before the age of 5, women living as virtual slaves, millennia of enforced ignorance and obedience to a small ruling class of kings and shamans.

Even today, with our watered-down post-Enlightenment version of the Village, hatred of gay people is practically a core Christian value, and we're still faced with irrational approaches to sex and reproduction, demands for obedience and money, and a worldwide sales force that goes out and squashes native cultures and installs tepid Village mush in their place.

On the other side, the side of the real world, we have accident victims brought back from the other side of death by the mundane miracles of medicine and surgery.

We have technology such that my voice and ears and eyes can reach halfway around the world to hold a simultaneous real-time discussion with a man in Australia, a kid in Pakistan, a woman in Scotland.

We have wealth and power and mobility in the hands of individuals, enough that I can drive across a continent in four days, fly across it in six hours.

We have light, so that I can sit up reading until 3 a.m.

We have comfort such that I can lie back in a soft chair in a warm, safe house and watch entertainment created by the cooperative effort of hundreds of people in far-flung locales.

None of which could ever be possible in the Village.

Not a tough choice.

Memories of our past

The Village will always be a part of our history. And it probably should be. As the place we grew up in and grew out of, it should be preserved in museums as part of our historical heritage ... but *only* our historical heritage.

I imagine a living history museum, complete with the dungeons and torture instruments, perhaps a handsome televangelist character trying to sell visitors a Healing Miracle Prayer Shawl so he could afford a ten-bedroom home with a six-car garage and an air-conditioned doghouse. The Perfect Hair Village Choir would sing about the miracles of the Mystic

Fairy Jesus and every visitor would be photographed standing next to the golden throne of the Big Magic Juju Guy.

It would be like those old Revolutionary War forts with costumed actors guiding us through and telling our story. Not to entice us back there, but to tell us: "This is the place where we grew up, that long preliminary moment in our history which we need to be reminded of so we can know how very lucky we are to be out of it."

As you go about your daily life, remember this: You are already an atheist.

If you're a Christian, or come from Christian roots, you are, in relation to the tenets of Islam, an atheist. You don't just not-know – in any consideration of Islam, you actively disbelieve in it. The value you place on it is less than zero.

In relation to the tenets of Shintoism, you're equally an atheist. The same is true of all your life and belief in relation to Zoroastrianism – you're an atheist.

Ditto for every other religion, living and dead, under the sun. If there's a Blue Stone of Heaven out there somewhere, once worshipped by some African jungle tribe (the idea of which I think I borrowed from an old Tarzan movie), then in relation to whatever lies and demands and unique practices they dreamed up for Blue-Stone-ism, you couldn't care less about them, because you're an atheist.

In fact, as a practical day-to-day matter, even if you're a devout Christian, you live your life *most of the time* as if you are an atheist. Even those who self-identify as Villagers spend most of their time in the real world, and so are functional atheists.

You don't pray when you flip on a light switch, though

people of previous eras would have seen the light that results as a godly miracle.

You don't genuflect and kiss the keyboard when you switch on your computer, even though the result of this sufficiently advanced technology seems magical. You don't offer up a silent ritual abasement when you turn the key in your car.

These things have nothing to do with prayer, and we all know it. They operate in a certain way, they *work*, because they were carefully made, with reason and science and technology, to function in a real-world way. The rest of your life, most of it, is the same way. And it works for you.

To take the next step is easier than you think. Casting off those last bits of reverence for the Village is just easy enough to do, just hard enough to be worth doing.

You don't have to give up the least scrap of your morality, your ethics, your security, your love of family or freedom. In fact, just the opposite – all of it becomes *more yours*.

All you have to give up is the illusion that those things come from an invisible giant in the sky.

The payoff in each life is worthwhile. Because, in my experience, once you get religion completely out of your head, amazing things start to happen. Understanding flows in. A quirky wide-ranging curiosity takes up residence. Childlike wonder blossoms. And a mental independence and self-confidence begins to grow, the conviction that you yourself can understand things, that you can make value judgments, that you don't have to refer every question of morality or reality to a priest or evangelist for direction.

But the payoff in society as a whole might be off the charts of anything we can imagine. With a critical mass of people exploring and learning totally outside the Village, we might create something revolutionary. Incredible things might start to happen.

We've already seen that revolution in the fields of science. In science, the distance between Greece's Golden Age and us is stunning.

But what if leaps of that same magnitude could be made in other fields? If advances as large as those we've made in physics and medicine could be made in morality? What would the world be like if we were as far beyond the Village in ethics as we are in biochemistry or nuclear physics?

What if there was a "vaccine" for poverty? What if a program to end ignorance was simpler to write than the million lines of code for a computer graphics program? What if ending starvation was easier than building an electron microscope? What if war was solvable in a way that made splitting the atom look unbelievably complex?

If you'll settle for nothing less than the opposite of adventure, the Village sits waiting for you. You can live your entire life in the comfortably familiar, and adventure will avoid you like the plague. You can walk down the same streets day after day after day, pretending that nothing will ever change, and grow more alienated from the rest of us each passing year as the world marches on beyond you.

But it's been *done*. That journey has been made by legions of people before you, in all of history and prehistory. The results are *known*.

For the greatest adventures of your life, for the greatest

discoveries of your life, you have to come Out Here, away from the Village.

Yes, there are discomforts to living in the real world. Adventure itself is uncomfortable – it's about camping on the ground, getting dunked in the river, getting lost. But it's also about seeing new things. Making discoveries. Having new ideas. Seeing sunrises from mountaintops. The rewards of adventure are frequently fantastic.

Yes, there are problems out here. But they are problems that are understandable and manageable. You don't have to try to read the inscrutable mind of an unpredictable sky-daddy. You don't have to fumble around in the dark murk of an opaque holy book looking for answers. You don't have to believe that priests and mystics are always brighter than you, more connected than you, and that only they have the answers.

Whether we know it or not, the answers have always come from us, and us alone. The question is, will we allow robed con men – who are, like us, still only human – to steal away our options by ordering us to take this road or that, actions that will benefit *them*? Or will we learn to make our own choices?

We start by clearing away the fog.

As for the rest, on our own, and with the help of our fellow thinking humans, we'll figure something out. We always do.

Because – as most of us know, most of the time, in all of our real world affairs – there's nobody here to do it but us.

HANK FOX

Into the Future

HANK FOX

24

Selling Unbelief

I've been accused a time or two of being a "fundamentalist atheist" for the strength of my views on the subject. I point out each time that there really can't be any such thing as a fundamentalist atheist.

By definition, for there to be fundamentalists there has to be, first, some sort of original text on which a belief is based; second, a progression of practices and principles which veer from that original text; and third, someone who rebels from all the laxness and demands that practices and principles go back to the "fundamental" meaning of the original text. Or at least what they think it is.

Since there is not and never has been any original "bible" of atheism, none of that stuff can happen. It is impossible to "fundamentalize" atheism. There may be loud atheists, there may be assertive atheists, there may be angry atheists, but there can be no fundamentalist atheists.

But to tell you the truth, I wish there *was* some kind of basic atheist text – an atheist primer which was widely-enough accepted to serve as a source book for training new atheists. A published map to guide you out of the clutches of religion.

Most atheists I've spoken to squirm when I bring something like this up, insisting that everybody has to get there on their own – and proselytizing will just create a new type of brainless and uncritical believer.

And I agree. Some or all will "believe" because you've told them to believe, rather than because they've learned to think on their own. Rather than turn their minds toward an honest examination of their inherited faith and then, through an individual act of magnificent mental revolution, deliberately declare their independence from beliefs enforced upon them from outside, they will simply accept what you tell them.

Atheism is a "conversion" like no other, because it is almost always an individual passage, and most often totally without outside aid, comfort or mentors. Rather than happening overnight in some sort of explosion of "born-again" bliss, it might take an extended period of healthy skepticism and careful thought to pass into this type of mental adulthood.

But I wish it wasn't so. Why should something so important be so lacking in ready assistance?

Consider this: An individual from a religious background can arrive at atheism in several distinctly different ways.

There are those who, in a fit of youthful rebellion, declare themselves atheists in order to piss off their parents. Or, more kindly, those who do it to grow and explore their own unique identities, apart from their parents. Call them Rebellion Atheists.

There are those who actually believe in their sect's god on some level, but after suffering some negative incident they believe might have been prevented by that god, they come to hate him. Call them Revenge Atheists.

As I said earlier, you will occasionally hear people claim "I used to be an atheist, but now I'm a devout Christian." These people are likely one of these first two kinds of atheists (assuming they're being honest, that is, about having once been atheists). Such people self-identify as atheists for a time, but they never really understand the philosophical underpinnings of it, or the grander implications.

Then there are the people who have performed that "magnificent mental revolution." I like to think of them as Awakened Atheists.

This is not some shabby trick that is susceptible to revision. Once you pry open your own eyes, you don't just close them again – not for anybody or anything. (Although you might be moved to the occasional drink, after you see what you see.)

Note the basic difference between the categories. The first two are what I might call "arrival atheists." They mistake atheism for a target, and they get there as fast as possible by skipping over all the intervening steps. They're like the guy who pays somebody to take a test for him – as if a good grade was more important than learning.

But the third type is a "journey atheist," the man or woman

who finds the value of becoming an atheist in the trip itself. He/she takes one thought at a time, one claim at a time, one conclusion at a time, and makes a gradual transition to unbelief, discovering new and beautiful philosophical scenery at every step along the way.

If you wanted to collect together a group of truly characteristic atheists, you'd aim for these journey atheists – thoughtful, never-give-up people who run the gauntlet of their culture's religious superstitions and fight their way from lies to light.

As I've said several times here, my own trip took years. Most of the time, I didn't even know I was on the road. I would find myself worrying at some religious idea and then suddenly come to a bright mental vista: "Hey, there never was any Garden of Eden! Adam and Eve really never existed! Those are just stories!" Or "Wow! You really don't have to be the least bit religious to be a good person!"

Looking back on it, I really am as proud of this accomplishment, this journey, as anything I've ever done. Becoming an atheist was the greatest single achievement of my young life. It was the moment when I knew I had grown up and become my own self.

But the trip to get there was confusing, it was difficult, it was damned *lonely*.

From this end of that journey, I can't help but ask myself how much easier things might have been if someone had just *told* me certain things – such as that you don't have to be goddy to be good.

Invariably, the squirm-factor comes back into play when I

mention this to fellow atheists. They say things like "Well, but becoming an atheist is a deeply personal journey. If they accept it only because we tell them to, it's no different than religion."

Well, yes. And no.

Let's say that in a diverse population of humans, there are three types of possible reactions to atheism.

First, there are those who just ain't ever gonna *get* it. They are mysteriously unable to question the things they are taught by the "authorities" in their lives, and they will be obedient to their home religions or superstitions their whole lives. You couldn't get them to understand the basics of atheism if you explained it with a children's pop-up book. Considering that none of us has infinite resources, it's probably better to leave these people alone.

Second, there are the hard-headed skeptics who will get there on their own. They will take the journey and undergo their own magnificent mental revolution. For them, there might be no need for help.

But then there's this third group: all those on the cusp of going one way or the other. Ah, *them* there might be good reason to approach.

Because once guided onto the path, there will be many who will make the journey and undergo their own magnificent mental revolution.

Yeah, there will be some silly rubes in this group who just uncritically and gullibly accept the basic ideas, completely failing to understand them. To them, the process will be no different from religion. They'll believe it because some authority *tells* them to believe it.

But even they just *might*, with the type of guidance I'm picturing, come to truly appreciate and understand what they have and start to see the grand implications that lie beyond atheism.

Considering the likelihood that many of these people might not find the path on their own, it seems careless of atheists not to reach out to them.

Living with the discomfort of indeterminacy when faced with a seemingly-important life choice, many of these people will sooner or later opt for some type or degree of religion. Because what choice will they have? Faced with a philosophical buffet that includes Religion 1, Religion 2, Religion 3, etc., with "freethought" or "atheism" nowhere on the menu, they'll end up picking from the available alternatives.

Worse, in any larger social or scientific issue where freethinkers and godders come to be at odds, these people will probably sit back and hold no strong position one way or the other. They'll tend to feel that, even if they personally do not ascribe to a religion, the forces of religion are generally benign and well-meaning, and perhaps deserve the benefit of the doubt.

So, they'll think, maybe schoolchildren *should* get exposed to the supposed moral effect of having the Ten Commandments posted in school hallways. Or, just for the sake of fairness, maybe "creation science" *should* be included in science textbooks. Or maybe gay marriage really *is* sinful, and stem cell research really *should* be stopped.

If we atheists and freethinkers truly want to live in a better world, it's a damned big mistake to simply assume good things are going to happen automatically. To assume that all those rugged mental individualists who are somehow "supposed" to become atheists will actually find the path, make the journey on their own, and then have enough energy left over to work on larger goals of justice, fairness and sanity.

Because to tell you the truth, I'm not sure there *is* any such group as those innate skeptics. It seems to me that we identify them only in retrospect, and that it's never inevitable that any particular person will make the atheist journey. Trusting that they exist is really a kind of pocket religion – a belief in fate.

The strategy of waiting and trusting fate is a mistake. In fact, I don't think it's a strategy at all. More than anything, I believe it's a remnant of a long history of living alongside godders and knowing they would torture and kill you if you spoke out.

The practice is not some important basic aspect of atheism. It is simple inertia.

At this point, we atheists are still the equivalent of hunter-gatherers – we seem to simply expect that our social environment will somehow automatically supply sane compatriots when we need them, and we make little or no effort to grow them ourselves.

Invasion, USA

Meanwhile, in the United States at least, the social environment has recently and radically changed. The godders have suddenly become aggressive: they have moved into our territory – our nation – and started making it *theirs*. They have their own radio stations, their own publishing houses, their own talking heads on radio and TV, their own textbook committees, their own elected officials. They are, with great deliberation, reaching out to and bringing into their own little belief club large numbers of our armed forces.

I say it's long past time we moved beyond the hunter-gatherer stage and took up farming.

I think a bit of farming could grow a bumper crop of atheists. Because in some ways, I believe religion is really rather fragile. Intelligent, healthy people – especially young people – stretch automatically toward the warm sun of sanity and reality, and their own mental independence.

Yes, we'll face weeds. Maybe a few poison plants. But we'll end with a harvest of sunny, bright, flowering unbelievers to keep us all company and help us shape a sensible, sane and compassionate world for the lot of us to live in.

To put it another way ...

We atheists need to proselytize.

We need to preach. Sell. Take out ads. Put up billboards. Buy signs on the sides of city buses. Distribute pamphlets. Set up permanent outreach efforts to college and high school students.

We need to go door to door and say, "Pardon me, ma'am, but have you heard the word of no-god?"

25

Further Sources of Information & Support

I could list a thousand things here for you to read or hear or see, but there's really no need. If you start with any one of these publications, groups or web sites, you'll just naturally branch out and find your own answers. Happy hunting!

Reading List:

The Demon Haunted World: Science as a Candle in the Dark, Carl Sagan
The God Delusion, Richard Dawkins
The End of Faith: Religion, Terror and the Future of Reason, Sam Harris
Letter to a Christian Nation, Sam Harris
God is Not Great: How Religion Poisons Everything, Christopher Hitchens
Irreligion: A Mathematician Explains Why the Arguments for God Just Don't Add Up, John Allen Paulos
Atheism: The Case Against God, George H. Smith

Evolution and the Myth of Creationism: A Basic Guide to the Facts in the Evolution Debate, Tim M. Berra

Atheist Universe: Why God Didn't Have a Thing to Do With It, David Mills

Darwin's Dangerous Idea, Daniel C. Dennett

The God Who Wasn't There (DVD), Brian Flemming, et. al.

Letting Go of God (CD), Julia Sweeney

Skeptical Inquirer (magazine)

Skeptic (magazine)

American Atheist (magazine)

Websites:

Blue Collar Atheist	www.blue-collar-atheist.com
Richard Dawkins	www.richarddawkins.net
Sam Harris	www.samharris.org
P.Z. Myers' *Pharyngula*	scienceblogs.com/pharyngula
The Friendly Atheist	friendlyatheist.com
Positive Atheism	www.positiveatheism.org
The Talk Origins Archive	www.talkorigins.org
List of Logical Fallacies	en.wikipedia.org/wiki/List_of_fallacies

Organizations:

Secular Student Alliance	www.secularstudents.org
Council for Secular Humanism	www.secularhumanism.org
American Atheists	www.atheists.org
Skeptics Society	www.skeptic.com
Atheist Meetup groups near you	www.atheists.meetup.com

To order additional copies of *Red Neck, Blue Collar, Atheist*, look for the order link at:

Hank Fox Books	www.hankfoxbooks.com
Blue Collar Atheist	www.blue-collar-atheist.com

HANK FOX